MULTINATIONALS: THE SWEDISH CASE

THE CROOM HELM SERIES IN INTERNATIONAL
BUSINESS
Academic Editor: Alan M. Rugman, Dalhousie University

Multinationals and Transfer Pricing
Alan M. Rugman and Lorraine Eden

MULTINATIONALS: THE SWEDISH CASE

Erik Hörnell and Jan-Erik Vahlne

ST. MARTIN'S PRESS
New York

© 1986 Erik Hörnell and Jan-Erik Vahlne
All rights reserved. For information, write:
St. Martin's Press, Inc., 175 Fifth Avenue,
New York, NY 10010
First published in the United States of America in 1986

Library of Congress Cataloging in Publication Data

Hörnell, Erik, 1943–
Multinationals: the Swedish case.

  Bibliography: p.
  Includes index.
  1. Corporations, Swedish.   2. Investments, Swedish.
3. Sweden—economic conditions.   I. Vahlne, Jan-Erik,
1941–   .   II. Title.
HD2883.H67   1986   338.8′89485   85-14581
ISBN 0-312-55258-0

Printed and bound in Great Britain

CONTENTS

PREFACE

As will be evident from the following pages, Swedish outward foreign direct investment increased strongly from the 1950s onwards. Partly because this outflow was not balanced by inward investments, and partly for other reasons, the labour unions questioned the impact of foreign direct investment and demanded an investigation by the government. A committee was appointed — the Committee on Foreign Direct Investment (DIRK) — whose members represented the most important interest-groups in Sweden: industry, unions, farmers and consumers. The authors of this book served as Assistant Secretary and Secretary respectively. The Committee started its work in early 1978.

The Committee's assignment, in accordance with its directives, was to study empirically the impact of inflows and outflows of foreign direct investment and their effects on the competitiveness of Swedish industry, technological development, employment, exports and industrial structure. Five major studies were undertaken (see Chapter 6) in which a variety of methods were applied. A concluding report (SOU, 1983:17) was written and submitted to the government in 1983. Part Two of this book has much in common with the report. Consequently, a majority of the Committee stands behind the conclusions arrived at and the policy recommendations given.

We consider that the Swedish experience and the impact of foreign direct investment on its society is also of interest to foreign students of multinational companies. Sweden is a small, open economy and the home country of a substantial number of multinationals dominating domestic industry. The methodological approach may also be of some interest.

Alf Carling, Mats Forsgren and Peter Sandén offered a lot of valuable criticism in their role as consultants to DIRK. This volume owes a lot to them but, of course, we (and the Committee) are also indebted to many others — too many to thank individually.

For dedicated work on the final text we would like to thank our secretaries Vanja Ekberg, Ingrid Rosenvinge, Gertrud Wollin, and our translator David Canter.

Erik Hörnell
Jan-Erik Vahlne
Institute of International Business
Stockholm School of Economics

FIGURES

Figures

TABLES

Tables

PART ONE:

THE SWEDISH MULTINATIONALS: DESCRIPTION AND
THEORY

1 SWEDEN: A SMALL OPEN ECONOMY

In the middle of the nineteenth century, Sweden was an extremely poor agricultural society, somewhat isolated from the rest of Europe. Today, Sweden is a heavily industrialised country, with an economy which is highly dependent on international exchange. A major proportion of Swedish industry, especially where foreign sales are concerned, is based on the multinational companies, numbering just over 100, covered by this book. In this first chapter, we shall describe the main characteristics of the Swedish economy, setting the scene for the expansion of Swedish multinational companies and the achievement of their current position. Quite a few of them had their roots in the latter

Table 1.1: Basic Statistics about Sweden

The Land			
Area (1,000 sq km)	450	Inhabitants in major cities, incl. suburbs (end of 1982), thousands:	
Lakes	9 %		
Arable area	7 %	Stockholm	1,402
		Gothenburg	694
Woodland	51 %	Malmö	453
The People			
Population (end of 1982), thousands		8,327	
Number of inhabitants per sq km		19	
Net natural increase (Average 1978–82), thousands		4	
Production			
Gross domestic product in 1982 (Skr billion)	623	Gross fixed capital formation in 1982, per cent of GDP	18.8
GDP per head, US $	11,909	Employment (1982) thousands	4,200
		Percentage of total:	
		Agriculture, fisheries	5.1
		Industry	23.7
		Other	71.2
The Currency			
Monetary unit: Krona			
Currency unit per US $, average of daily figures 1983: 7.67			

Source: *OECD Economic Survey* (1984)

3

part of the nineteenth century and the great expansion of foreign activities took place, at an increased tempo, after the Second World War. The new situation which we face today, with serious problems of balance in Swedish economy, is the picture which we have to use when evaluating the future development of the multinational companies.

How It All Started[1]

The industrialisation of Sweden started rather late, especially in comparison with Great Britain, which was first in the field. In fact, it was the industrialisation of Great Britain and the subsequent expansion of construction investments that initiated Swedish industrialisation. Although Sweden possessed natural resources in the form of iron ore, forests and water, there were no domestic forces capable of starting up the industrial development process since Sweden was a small country with a largely agricultural population.

The expansion of building and construction activities in Great Britain meant a substantial increase in the demand for timber products which could only be supplied from abroad. This created an enormous boom for the Swedish wood-products industry in the period 1850–80. In addition, industrialisation in other parts of Europe led to increased demand for Sweden's traditional export products, iron and steel, where Sweden had an important comparative advantage in the form of access to energy (charcoal). Forest products, iron and steel jointly comprised more than half of Swedish exports at this time while a further third was represented by agricultural products, mainly oats, which were used to feed the more than 250,000 horses used for transport in London. Great Britain was the destination of almost half of the Swedish export total and was quite clearly the dominant export market up until the outbreak of the Second World War. Today, Great Britain shares the role of leading export market with Germany and Norway — each of these three countries represents rather more than 10 per cent of Swedish exports.

The production of the original Swedish export products, iron, steel and timber products, required close proximity to raw materials and energy sources. Production was based on numerous small units which had no direct contacts with foreign markets — exports were arranged by merchant houses in Stockholm and Gothenburg, the major ports. Some of these merchant houses were founded by British businessmen; their personnel could speak foreign languages and were well acquainted with foreign markets. Furthermore, these merchant houses had access to capital, which was an advantage since the Swedish banking system was relatively undeveloped at this time. Wood and iron exports gave the merchants good returns, which were later used to finance the establishment of new industrial companies. The import of capital was also a significant factor in Swedish development although such imported finance was mainly used for investments in infrastructure, for example in railways.

When the demand for timber products finally began to slow down, the forest output was increasingly used on the manufacture of pulp and paper. New inventions made it possible to produce paper exclusively from wood fibre. Technological developments in the production of iron and steel also had important consequences for Sweden — coke could now be used instead of charcoal, and iron ore with a high phosphorus content became a viable raw material. These developments meant that Sweden lost its advantage as a producer of ordinary commercial steel but could, on the other hand, export ore with a high phosphorus content from the north of the country. Swedish iron and steel works began to switch from the production of commercial steel to special steel, where Sweden achieved a dominant position. The move into special steels also meant that the Swedish works began to concentrate on products designed to meet purchaser requirements, thus involving the development of new sales channels.

The forming and processing of metals developed from iron and steel production and this, in turn, later became the basis for the Swedish engineering industry. The 1880s was probably the most creative period in the development of Swedish industry — many of today's major engineering multinationals were founded in this period, for example Alfa-Laval, Ericsson and ASEA. The innovations on which these companies were based often originated abroad but were then adapted and developed by Swedish engineers. The boom in the engineering industry was also based on a major investment in technological education and training where studies abroad played an important part — many Swedish engineers received their training abroad, especially in England. Thus, in this respect, too, impulses from outside the country were decisive in determining future development.

The new industrial companies, based on innovation, began to export and establish foreign contacts at an early stage. The travelling salesmen who prepared the way for the export success of Swedish companies played a vital, if not particularly glamorous, role in these developments. Ericsson, for example, employed an Englishman who travelled around Russia with telephones in his suitcase — he is said to have sold 600 telephones to a telephone exchange in Kiev in 1893. Ericsson, AGA and Alfa-Laval also established manufacturing operations abroad in the 1890s. Alfred Nobel's corporation, Nitroglycerin AB, had already started manufacturing in ten different countries in the 1870s. The next great wave of Swedish establishment abroad came in the boom of the 1920s. SKF was already the most internationalised company, although it had only started operations in 1907. By 1933 SKF was selling in 56 countries outside Sweden, had sales companies in 26 countries and manufacturing facilities in five countries; 60 per cent of SKF group employees were foreigners.

Sweden's non-participation in two world wars was, of course, a contributory factor in Sweden's successful economic development in the twentieth century. Swedish companies were able to supply goods for reconstruction abroad after both world wars since the Swedish production aparatus had not been destroyed. Furthermore, after the First World War Sweden was able, *de facto*, to write off a major proportion of its foreign debts as a result of foreign inflation. Sweden came relatively unscathed through the depression of the 1930s, since the Swedish krona was heavily undervalued after Sweden abandoned the gold standard in 1931.

The Golden Years

The decades immediately after the Second World War represented a period of record expansion for Swedish industry. In many respects, this stage in the development of the Swedish economy corresponds to the international picture. Restricted foreign trade, in the 1930s, and wartime embargoes meant that Swedish industry was not highly specialised in the late 1940s. There were two important reasons for the rapid increase in productivity that then took place. One reason was the increase in foreign trade resulting from the removal of trade barriers. Better and cheaper transport and freight also stimulated trade — although this was a negative factor for Swedish iron ore and paper pulp since the positional advantages were lost *vis-à-vis* transatlantic competitors.

The foundation of the EEC in 1957 and EFTA (of which Sweden is a member state) in 1960 played an important part in the internationalisation of Swedish industry. Sweden's position deteriorated *vis-à-vis* the EEC countries but incentives to trading with the Nordic countries within EFTA increased. As we will see in Chapter 3, many Swedish companies decided to set up production within the EEC in order to maintain and expand their sales in this region. Sweden later signed a free trade agreement with the EEC, but this did not come into effect until 1973 and tariffs were not completely abolished until 1977.

The second factor which was of great importance in increasing productivity was the so-called 'wage solidarity' which meant that wages and salaries were increased at about the same rate in all companies. This meant that the least productive companies were eliminated and that the labour force gradually moved to the more productive companies. The result was a greater increase in total industrial productivity than can be explained purely by increased investments and technological development linked with such investment.

In the mid-1960s, Sweden achieved an 'all-time high' share of world exports. However, Swedish companies began to meet severe and increased international competition. The main reason for the stiffening of the competitive climate was that other countries had now completed the reconstruction of their production capacity and, in fact, in many cases had more modern plants. In retrospect, some observers have maintained that Sweden did not push through a programme of structural change hard enough in the 1950s, since it was still possible to sell the output of inefficient production units while post-war demand remained at a high level. It has also been said that the investments which were undertaken were excessively aimed at increasing productivity and that more long-term or future-oriented investments were neglected. Companies concentrated too much on measures which improved productivity because wages for unskilled labour were relatively high. When, subsequently, global surplus capacity developed in many industries, Sweden was faced with several acute problems.

The New Situation

Although Sweden, as an industrial power, reached its peak in the mid-1960s, the country's relative decline did not become obvious until well into the 1970s. The turning point in the early 1970s is a phenomenon which affected several countries, but subsequent development has been worse in Sweden's case. The international recession of 1974–5 hit harder than any similar downturn in the post-war period. In Sweden's case, the negative effects of the recession were reinforced because certain key Swedish industries, such as shipbuilding, forest products and iron and steel, were especially affected. The market for 15–20 per cent of Swedish output practically disappeared after 1975.

Swedish economic policy aimed at expansion in order to maintain employment levels. When business improved in 1975, industry agreed to 40 per cent wage and salary increases in 1975–6. On top of everything, the Swedish krona was tied to the Deutschemark which meant that the krona was *de facto* revalued against most other currencies. The combined effect of wage increases and a more expensive krona was disastrous for the Swedish industry's international competitiveness. We shall return to these problems when we discuss the export effects of foreign investments.

In order to restore some sort of balance, the krona was devalued several times. It proved to be difficult, however, to regain market shares once they had been lost. Figure 1.1 shows that the development

Figure 1.1: Sweden's Comparative Economic Performance

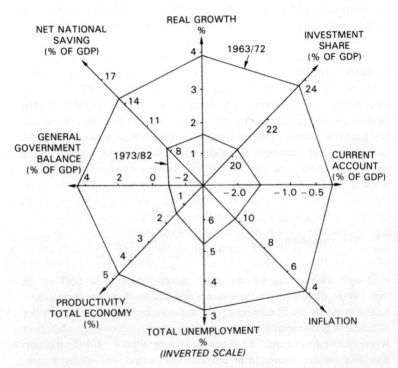

Source: *OECD Economic Survey* (1984), p. 8.

of the Swedish economy was worse in the 19731–82 period than in 1968–73, whichever economic indicator we use. Combining the goals of maintaining employment while avoiding excessive inflationary and external deficit problems has become increasingly hard.

Swedish industry has not only lost market shares abroad but has suffered in the domestic market, too. Industrial production was 10 per cent lower in 1982 than in the peak year of 1974 and investments in fixed assets have also declined.[2] Investments by Swedish industry in research and development and marketing are, when combined, of roughly the same order as physical investments. Research and development and marketing investments are, in turn, of roughly equal volume. It is more difficult to determine the volume of foreign investments, since the information available covers investments financed directly from Sweden but does not include investments via subsidiaries. However, it is estimated that foreign investments by the 18 largest Swedish multinationals corresponded to 40 per cent of total industrial investment in Sweden in 1982.[3]

Swedish Exports

In common with many other small countries, Sweden is heavily dependent on foreign trade. Even as far back as the 1870s, Swedish exports were 20 per cent of GNP and, over the years, this proportion has increased to around 30 per cent. Since the service sector and, above all, the public sector have grown most in recent decades, it is more appropriate to compare foreign trade with the proportion of GNP attributable to the value added in the physical goods sector. If the export of goods is compared with economic activities 1–4 in the ISIC system, we find that the proportion of GNP attributable to the export of goods has increased from 45 per cent in the mid-1950s to approximately 80 per cent in the early 1980s (Alvstam and Lundin, 1983, p. 199).

If we look at changes in the export of physical goods, we find that they reflect the restructuring of Swedish industry which has taken place. Engineering products represented about one third of the total in 1960 and then increased rapidly until the mid-1970s, when their share was 50 per cent (see Figure 1.2). The losers have been the forest products and basic metal sectors. In the case of the forest industry the decline has primarily involved wood products and pulp, while paper has maintained its export share. Broadly speaking, the entire deterioration in the mining and metal sector can be explained in terms of a drop in iron ore

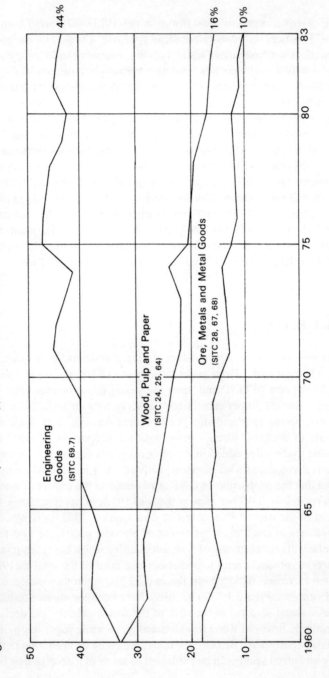

Figure 1.2: Shares of Some Important Types of Goods in Swedish Exports (%)

Engineering
Goods
(SITC 69.7)

Wood, Pulp and Paper
(SITC 24, 25, 64)

Ore, Metals and Metal Goods
(SITC 28, 67, 68)

44 %

16 %

10 %

1960   65   70   75   80   83

50   40   30   20   10

Source: Adapted from Alvstam and Lundin (1983)

exports. Thus, it is not difficult to conclude that raw materials have lost export shares, while more sophisticated products have gained. This picture is, in fact, roughly the same for all industrialised countries but the change has perhaps been more wide-sweeping in Sweden, since Sweden has previously been unusually heavily dependent on exports of raw materials.

Although Swedish exports have come to be increasingly dominated by more advanced products, consumer goods represent rather less than 20 per cent of the total. Swedish exports are thus mainly a question of components and investment goods — products used in production. More than half the exports of engineering products are capital goods (see Figure 1.3) and consequently Swedish engineering exports are heavily dependent on investment developments in foreign markets. Export sales also tend to lag somewhat behind the overall business cycle, both in upturns and recessions.

Figure 1.3: Composition of Swedish Exports of Engineering Goods, 1983 (%)

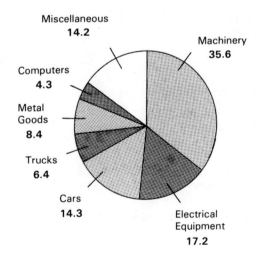

Source: *Verkstadsindustrins konjunkturläge* (1984: 2)

Although exports are sold to a great many different countries, the original heavy concentration on Nordic and Western European countries is still a dominant factor. Figure 1.4 indicates a change in engineering exports between 1969 and 1983. Although engineering exports to OPEC, Eastern Asia and North America show the most marked increases, Western Europe, which takes 60 per cent of Swedish exports, is in a class of its own. If we look at the pattern for all types of Swedish exports, we find that the Western European share is almost 70 per cent. The country-of-destination statistics have been remarkably constant in the post-war period — OPEC represents the major increase of exports while the exports to Latin America have stagnated. In both cases, however, the changes are relatively small, seen against a background of total Swedish exports.

Figure 1.4: Exports of Engineering Goods to Different Regions in 1969 and 1983 (1983 prices; Skr billion)

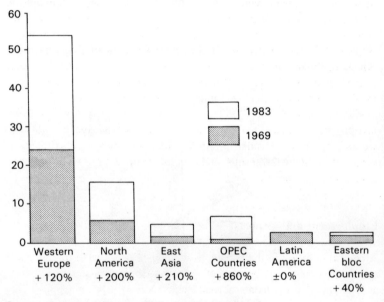

Source: *Verkstadsindustrins konjunkturläge* (1984: 2)

Notes

1. The major sources for this section have been Carlson (1979), Hallvarsson (1980) and Heckscher (1936).
2. Industry, however, now tends to use plant and manufacturing facilities owned by leasing or construction companies to a greater extent and therefore statistics describing industrial investment may be misleading.
3. Veckans affärer (1984:16)

2   THE DEBATE ABOUT MULTINATIONALS

This chapter contains a brief survey of questions which have surfaced in the debate concerning multinationals and foreign direct investments. The economic effects which we will analyse more thoroughly later in this book are: structure of industry, employment, exports, technical development and the Swedish industries' international competitiveness. These effects do not, however, cover all the questions which have been debated and discussed as a result of increased foreign direct investment. In fact, some of the most controversial topics are not dealt with at all in the present assignment.

The debate which has taken place in Sweden has been mainly concerned with the outflow of direct investments since these have been considerably greater than the inflow of investments in the 1970s. The effects of the direct investment outflow on the home country has been primarily discussed in Great Britain, Sweden and the United States, while in other countries, and in international organisations in general, the major emphasis has been placed on the effects on the host country where the investment takes place. In the following coverage of the economic debate, we wish firstly to consider questions which will later be illustrated by means of the empirical results, and then to comment on some of the other controversial issues.

Employment and Exports

A central question in the debate, which has been initiated by the trade union movement, has been whether employment in Sweden is falling as a result of investments abroad made by Swedish companies. The underlying assumption in this question is that multinational companies would have been able to locate a larger proportion of their investments in Sweden by reducing their profitability requirements, which would then have led to higher exports and employment in industry. At the international trade union movement level, there has been a discussion about whether multinational companies invest in developing countries to exploit poor employee working conditions, high rates of unemployment and low trade union membership figures.

The effects of the input of direct investments on employment have

13

also been discussed. In this case, the central point has been whether security of employment in the subsidiaries of multinational companies in Sweden is reduced as a result of the difficulties experienced by employees and the authorities in influencing the central planning function in foreign companies. It has also been maintained that those responsible for decisions in foreign companies do not feel sufficiently strong ties with Sweden and Swedish society and have insufficient understanding of the social consequences of a decision to shut down a plant or to cease operations.

In the United States, there has been some discussion of whether the slight net effect on employment which may perhaps be ascribed to direct investments actually disguises a greater, gross change, which leads to the creation of an appreciable number of jobs demanding a high level of competence, while also leading to the disappearance of many unskilled jobs. This line of thinking also enters into the discussion of effects on the regional industrial structure. An important factor leading to negative attitudes towards structural change is that such changes often imply both retraining and relocation for employees.

Technical Development

The possible significance of multinational companies in creating and spreading the technical know-how which is of such great importance for Swedish industrial development, is another important question which has been much discussed. In principle, a favourable result of the establishment of foreign-owned companies should be the transfer of technical know-how within international enterprises. From the Swedish point of view, however, it is sometimes questioned whether the establishment of foreign subsidiaries by Swedish companies does not also, in the long run, lead to the increased localisation of research and development activities abroad.

The fears which have been voiced about the inflow of direct investments in this connection have involved certain technologically advanced Swedish companies which have been purchased by foreign interests. Yields from the technical experience and know-how which have been created in the host country then become an asset for the international corporation. The risk of the transfer abroad of research and development activities in the company which has been taken over has also been pointed out — it has been suggested that the Swedish operations are then likely to shift towards simpler objectives and assignments.

Growth and Efficiency

As already implied, those who question foreign investments in terms of employment effects assume that there are not any decisive differences in profitability between investments in the home country and abroad. Industry has, however, maintained that the positive effects of doing business at an international level have been seriously underestimated. Economic development and higher living standards in Sweden are, in fact, very much dependent on the existence of international operations. Direct investments are regarded as one element in a process of international specialisation where each country uses its resources in an optimal manner — to produce goods where the country in question has a comparative advantage in manufacturing. Industry has, however, been aware that the foreign investments of Swedish companies cause certain adjustment and balancing problems but it is considered that these difficulties have been relatively insignificant compared with the problems caused by changes in the business cycle and other similar factors.

Competition, Company Structure and Regional Balance

Many battles have been fought over the question of the extent to which multinational companies influence competitive conditions and company structures both in international trade and in national markets. One line of thought holds that the very existence of multinational companies leads to increased competition, while others think that such companies eliminate competition. The drawbacks ascribed to multinational companies apply to some extent to all large corporations, although the problem may be accentuated since the multinational companies tend to dominate in certain key industries, characterised by differentiated products and rapid growth.

The debate about whether the existence of multinational companies leads to reduced competition tends to evolve into the discussion of a number of sub-problems. One such sub-problem is whether overall group management in multinational corporations determines what the various subsidiaries are to manufacture and export, thus possibly having unfavourable effects on the host country in the form of increased dependence on imports or poor exploitation of the country's resources. Another such question concerns whether multinational companies contribute to the establishment of increased price levels. The thought in the background here is that multinational corporations often work in markets characterised by limited competition or oligopoly.

A third area of interest has been increased industrial concentration, resulting from the purchase of domestic companies by international concerns. A fourth problem, in the area of limitation of competition, involves agreements to share markets, discriminatory pricing and other restrictions linked with licensing agreements between multinational and domestic companies.

Yet another question which has been discussed in this connection is whether the growth of direct investments and of multinational companies makes it more difficult to start up and operate cooperative business and industrial activities on a national or regional basis. In this connection, it has been pointed out that the concentration of production within a few large companies will result in a reduction in the choice of potential suppliers and increased difficulties in starting up competitive production operations.

The question of whether the multinational companies' large-scale activities counteract the ambition to have a varied industrial structure in different parts of the country is another controversial issue. Increased economies of scale in production, combined with lower transport costs, tend to lead to a concentration of manufacturing and a reduced number of production units. Product development, in turn, requires proximity to centres of higher education and concentration on major sales areas. Indeed, concentration and economies of scale are factors to be taken into account in such typically home market industries such as bakeries, breweries and flour mills. What is relevant for the discussion — or should be relevant — is, therefore, the extent to which international investments tend to increase problems which are already present in the economy.

Consumer Interests

There has been considerable discussion of the question of whether the expansion of multinational companies has been in the interest of the consumer or not. It has been questioned whether direct investments really lead to more efficient production, which then benefits the consumer in the form of lower prices. It has been pointed out that a dominant market position for the multinationals may lead to increased oligopolistic pricing, cartels and other agreements which raise consumer price levels. It has also been suggested that multinational companies may influence product design in a broad sense. On the one hand, the multinationals have the resources to undertake more rapid product development while, on the other hand, the physical distance between consumption and production tends to increase. The separation between consumption and production means, for example, that consumers are less likely to see specific needs satisfied and met and they find it more difficult to express their views.

In Sweden a national agency is responsible for looking after consumer interests. When an international corporation establishes itself in a new country, these authorities are faced with a more powerful counterpart in negotiations than when they dealt with an agent or importer. The multinational concern's international roots, mobility, contact network and resources make it more able to control development in accordance with its interests than would be the case for a purely national company. An example often mentioned in the course of discussion is that international corporations have influenced the preparation of international standards and specifications, for example for consumer products.

Trade Union Activities

Both in Sweden and internationally, the trade union movement has expressed anxiety that, as the company becomes more international, unions will be increasingly less able to defend their members' interests satisfactorily. The unions have therefore proposed increased international cooperation to counteract the strong negotiating position which the multinational corporations are supposed to have. The Swedish unions, however, do not consider that the multinationals have pursued anti-union policies. The problem is said, instead, to be that the multinational companies may weaken union activities in countries with a strong trade union tradition by concentrating their activities in parts of the world where unions are weak and divided. This would then mean that expansion in countries with weak unions would take place at the cost of employment in strong union countries, thus undermining the basis for healthy union activities.

The opportunities which multinational companies have to allocate production between various countries may also appear to restrict the opportunities of pursuing aggressive union policies in any single country. Merchant shipping has been mentioned as an extreme example of high mobility across national borders. The transfer of a vessel to another national flag can rapidly change conditions of work and terms of payment on board, thus reducing the opportunities for union activities at a national level.

In principle, the same disadvantages may occur in the working environment as for wages and other conditions of employment. The special problem in multinational companies is that new products and new production processes are often developed at a central level. These production processes then filter down to the corporations' various subsidiaries. This leaves the local union organisations with no more than the possibility of intervening at a late stage in an attempt to correct or modify what may be a poorly designed production process.

A characteristic of multinationals is that they have a more impenetrable structure than that of national companies. It is therefore said to be difficult for the employees to approach and influence the real decision-makers. When union representatives wish to negotiate on a particular question, local management can refer to group management in another country. It has been suggested that this is one reason why negotiations can be problematical and protracted.

Another alleged result of this impenetrable structure is that the trade unions may receive inadequate financial information. Negotiations may therefore be characterised by uncertainty as to how the results of the negotiations will influence an organisation's future plans. Similarly, in wage and salary negotiations, it may be difficult to determine whether the accounts presented for the various subsidiaries are fair. Low profits in a subsidiary may be the result, for example, of high transfer prices paid to the parent company.

It has also been pointed out that a multinational corporation is able to apply various contract periods for various sections of the group organisation. This means that top central management is not obliged to negotiate for the whole organisation simultaneously. Multinational companies are also said to be able to take what may be termed disguised combative action by rearranging production between subsidiaries in various countries, thus creating an impression that the flow of incoming orders has deteriorated and employment is threatened. If there is a dispute in one country, the organisation can reduce the negative effects of such an industrial conflict by increasing production in other subsidiaries.

Swedish trade unionists have also maintained that security of employment in the multinational companies is not necessarily above average, despite the fact that these companies often achieve higher profitability than other companies. The reason is said to be that multinational companies are better equipped to conduct rapid structural rationalisation within the total organisation. Where a national company with low profits would still continue operations, due to a lack of alternatives, a multinational company can disinvest or move to a country with higher profit yields relatively quickly. The multinational companies are therefore said to take a more short-term view than their national equivalents, since they react in a dramatic manner when faced with problems which may be temporary.

Taxation

It is commonly believed that multinationals pay less tax than national companies. It is assumed that international concerns prefer to manipulate their profits so that they show up in subsidiaries in countries with low company taxation. Tax havens are especially mentioned in this connection — countries with low or no company taxation.

Another question here is the extent to which differences in corporate taxation in different countries influence or steer the setting up of production activities by multinational companies. Certain countries use tax relief or other subsidies to attract new foreign enterprise, which has caused increasing irritation in international relations.

Social and Cultural Effects

In addition to the economic effects of multinational company activities on society, there has also been some discussion of the influence of direct investments on social and cultural patterns. Such discussion has mainly taken the situation of developing countries as its starting point. It is said that the technology and the products introduced by multinationals may have negative effects on the host country's cultural identity and social structure. There has been special reference to increased investments from multinational breweries and tobacco companies in developing countries at a time when demand in the industrialised world is stagnant.

The activities of two multinational Swiss companies have given rise to the most emotional debates on this theme. One of the companies is Nestlé, whose sales of mother's-milk substitutes are said to increase infant mortality in developing countries. The other example is CIBA-Geigy, whose sales of a gastric medicine, oxichinolin, are forbidden in Sweden and other Western countries, but permitted in developing countries. Other pharmaceutical manufacturers are also accused of dumping prohibited drugs in developing countries.

Conclusions

Foreign direct investments by companies involve a degree of conscious integration between the countries affected. Sweden's increased dependence on foreign countries should therefore perhaps be seen as an overall consequence or effect of such direct investments. This increased dependence means reduced freedom of action in the field of economic policy, but can also involve limitations and restrictions in other areas, such as union and consumer affairs. There is, in addition, difficulty in obtaining information and insight into the activities of multinationals. These companies have acquired a reputation for being anonymous and amorphous, which has been a source of anxiety. In brief, we can therefore summarise by saying that the debate has been centred on the various consequences of the fact that companies can operate over national borders, while the countries' opportunities for gaining insight and taking action are limited to their own national territory.

3 THE STRUCTURE OF SWEDISH MULTINATIONALS

This chapter describes some major characteristics of the structure of Swedish multinational companies. We shall present information illustrating the origins, size, expansion and field of operation of these companies. Most of the information has been collected by the Swedish government's Committee on Foreign Direct Investments and covers the 1965–78 period. Some of the figures have been subsequently updated on the basis of company balance sheets and other published statistics.

Flows of In- and Outward Foreign Direct Investment

Since Sweden is a relatively small market, it might have been anticipated that foreign companies would be less interested in manufacturing in Sweden than Swedish companies would be in production abroad. In the 1960s, however, investments by foreign companies in Sweden were roughly of the same order as Swedish companies' investments abroad. In fact, in a couple of years the inflow of direct investments was actually greater than the outflow. The relatively large input of investments can be explained by the hypothesis that Sweden was regarded, especially by American companies, as a test market for consumer products prior to a broader launch in the rest of Europe. Another explanation is that Sweden had relatively low wages for skilled labour.

Something happened in the late 1960s which changed the trend, however. From 1969 onwards, the outflow of direct investments started to increase dramatically, while the inflow was stable at the same level as previously. By 1974, the investment outflow was three times as large as the inflow and by 1977 six times as large (see Figure 3.1). This remarkable development coincided with a period when the Swedish economy was suffering from the serious balance of trade problems which have been described in Chapter 1. In the period 1979–83, however, the inflow of direct investments increased almost as fast as the outflow, largely as a result of the purchase of several Swedish companies by foreign interests.

Figure 3.1: Permits of In- and Outward Foreign Direct
Investments, 1973–83, (Skr million current prices,
logarithmic scale)

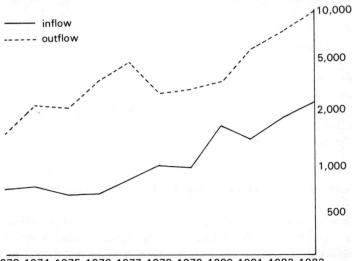

Source: The Central Bank of Sweden.

Where and When Did the Establishment of Foreign Operations Take Place?

We define a multinational company as an industrial enterprise with at
least one manufacturing subsidiary abroad. Our definition is somewhat
narrower than that used by the Central Bank of Sweden for foreign direct
investment. The Bank's concept also includes investments in pure sales
companies, as well as investments in non-industrial activities, such as
insurance. Using our definition, there were 118 Swedish multinational
companies in 1978. These companies controlled 570 manufacturing subsidiaries abroad, in addition to 1,054 pure sales companies (see Table
3.1). Swedish multinationals had a total of roughly 300,000 employees
abroad, three-quarters of them working for subsidiaries with some form
of manufacturing activity. We have established a further limit here in
stipulating that production must amount to at least 10 per cent of the
sales of these subsidiaries' total sales value. This means that manufacturing subsidiaries should not be seen purely as production units but that,
in varying degrees, they pursue sales activities for the Swedish company group. Subsidiaries are defined as companies where the Swedish

Table 3.1: The Foreign Subsidiaries of the Swedish Multinational Groups, 1965, 1970, 1974 and 1978

	Number of Subsidiaries				Number of Employees			
	1965	1970	1974	1978	1965	1970	1974	1978
Manufacturing subsidiaries	329	428	481	570	147,810	182,650	219,620	227,825
Sales subsidiaries	464	674	892	1,054	22,440	36,130	49,665	53,695
Subsidiaries with other activities	na	na	64	68	780	3,665	15,520	19,690
Total	793	1,102	1,437	1,692	171,030	222,445	284,805	301,210

na Not available.
Source: SOU (1982:27).

group holds at least 50 per cent of the share capital.

As we have already noted in Chapter 1, several of today's multinationals moved into foreign markets at a very early stage. Table 3.2 indicates that there were more than 50 manufacturing subsidiaries abroad as early as the late 1920s. Most of today's major Swedish companies were already multinationals in the period of great economic prosperity that followed the Second World War. Almost half of the considerable number of subsidiaries founded subsequently were set up within the EEC. Two-thirds of the subsidiaries of Swedish multinationals were located in Western Europe in 1978, while only slightly more than 10 per cent were in North America.

Three-quarters of all subsidiaries were founded after 1960. Table 3.2 indicates that the number of subsidiaries set up was considerably greater in the 1970s than in the 1960s. However, we must note that the number of subsidiaries established in the 1960s was greater than the figures would appear to indicate, since a considerable number of companies set up before 1970 have been wound up or sold. This is indicated indirectly in the final column of Table 3.2 which categorises subsidiaries in existence in 1970 by date of foundation. Out of more than 400 subsidiaries listed in 1970, 30 per cent were later sold or discontinued. Thus there has been a significant change in the 'population' of subsidiaries.

The spread of Swedish subsidiaries over the various regions roughly corresponds with the distribution of Swedish exports. Western Europe and the developing countries, however, have a higher rating as regards exports than they achieve for the establishment of subsidiaries, while the reverse is true above all for Latin America, but also for North America. Differences in the spread of subsidiaries and of exports can be largely explained in terms of trade barriers. Latin America has consciously pursued a policy designed to favour domestic production and limit imports. The formulation of the EEC in the late 1950s also caused many Swedish companies to establish themselves within the Common Market tariff walls — it was not known at that time that Sweden would later sign a free trade agreement with the EEC.

Table 3.3 indicates the regional distribution of subsidiaries for various industries. Subsidiaries in the engineering and chemical industries have a global spread while other industries are only found in certain regions. In the vehicle industry (i.e. primarily Volvo), the establishment of foreign manufacturing facilities has largely been the result of a need to circumvent tariff barriers. In the case of the EEC, Latin America and North America, duties were higher for imports of finished vehicles than for knock-down kits and components. The only industry where foreign

Table 3.2: Time of Establishment and Location of Manufacturing Subsidiaries Still in Operation in 1978

Period of establishment	EEC	EFTA	Other Europe	North America	Other industrialised countries	Latin America	Other developing countries	All Regions	Subsidiaries in operation in 1970
1875–1919	8	6		3				17	(20)
1920–1929	15	4	3	1	1	6	1	31	(37)
1930–1939	9	5			2	2	1	19	(31)
1940–1949	2	4		2	4	10	1	23	(30)
1950–1959	20	4	1	7	1	12	1	46	(57)
1960–1965	38	10		6	3	9	5	71	(106)
1966–1970	45	17	6	8	3	10	2	91	(146)
1971–1974	59	26	4	14	5	7	3	118	
1975–1978	77	20	5	17	6	22	4	151	
Total	273	96	19	58	25	78	18	567	(427)

Source: SOU (1982:27).

Table 3.3: Employment in Manufacturing Subsidiaries in 1978, by Industry and Region

Distribution in %

Industry	EEC	EFTA	Other Europe	North America	Other industrialised countries	Latin America	Other developing countries	Total	Number of Employees
Food	96			4				100	2,174
Textile and clothing	13	78	8	1				100	4,583
Pulp and paper	73	16		11				100	8,707
Paper products and printing	59	15	1	16	2	7		100	12,314
Chemicals	33	17	1	13	1	27	8	100	17,031
Metal and metal goods	57	6	2	12	7	12	4	100	28,414
Machinery	68	5	1	13	2	8	3	100	77,515
Electrical goods	30	6	10	12	7	34	1	100	48,537
Transportation goods	54			2	3	39	2	100	18,057
Other industries	79	15	1	4		1		100	9,817
Number of employees	122,564	19,694	7,133	24,940	7,781	38,974	6,063		227,149

Source: SOU (1982:27)

investments have been definitely resource oriented is the clothing industry, where lower wages have been the primary reason for establishment abroad, mainly in Portugal and Finland. The paper/pulp industry also has a couple of production units in North America which are raw-material based.

Permits for direct investments abroad issued between 1979 and 1983 indicate that the establishment of manufacturing subsidiaries in Western Europe is declining (see Figure 3.2). The major increase has taken place in the United States — 26 per cent of total investments in the last five years. Figure 3.2 also indicates a fairly good tally between different countries' share of the Swedish outflow of direct investments and the proportion of foreign direct investments coming into Sweden. However, it should be noted that the outflow of investments has been more than four times as large as the inflow since 1979. Although the United States represents, quite clearly, the major proportion of the investment inflow, American investors no longer have total dominance. If we take the 1962–75 period, the inflow of American investments was almost four times larger than investments from Britain, the next largest source. Today, roughly a third of the inflow of direct investments comes from other Nordic countries — above all from Finnish companies, which appear to regard Sweden as a suitable take-off point in their internationalisation process.

Small and Large Multinationals

Despite the dramatic increase in the number of subsidiaries in recent decades, the number of Swedish companies with foreign production facilities has only increased from 82 in 1965 to 118 in 1978. Furthermore, the major increase took place before 1970. If we then examine the 118 companies with foreign subsidiaries in 1978, we find that only 47 (or approximately 40 per cent) had manufacturing operations abroad throughout the whole period from 1965 to 1978. It is, however, this smaller group of companies, multinational throughout the period, which dominates the operations of Swedish companies abroad. Furthermore, we should note that the 20 largest companies within this group employ more than 80 per cent of all employees working for foreign subsidiaries.

Who are the new multinationals? Most of them are relatively small companies — 64 of the 118 multinationals had fewer than 2,000 employees (SOU, 1984:6, p. 14). These 64 small multinationals

Figure 3.2: Permits of In- and Outward Foreign Direct Investments, 1979–83, by Host and Home Country

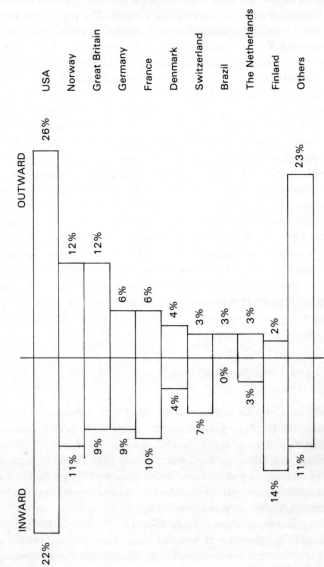

Source: The Central Bank of Sweden

represented less than 3 per cent of the total value-added figure for Swedish industry. The remaining 54 multinationals, with more than 2,000 employees, were responsible for 65 per cent of the value-added total. The small multinationals are often specialised high-technology companies which rapidly achieve appreciable foreign sales and also start manufacturing facilities abroad a few years after their original foundation. Hence multinationalism is not something that can only be associated with large companies. On the other hand, if we wish to describe the foreign direct investment phenomenon and Swedish industry's foreign operations, the group of 20 or 30 major multinationals dominates the total picture.

Appendix A contains a brief presentation of the 20 largest Swedish multinationals in 1983 and gives figures for the number of employees, foreign sales and export shares. Swedish multinationals have characteristically selected a strategy in which they attempt to specialise and become world leaders in limited product areas where quality, service and knowledge of the market are more important competitive tools than price. Ericsson is one of the world's five largest companies in the telecommunications equipment field, SKF is the world's largest manufacturer of ball bearings with a 20 per cent world market share, Electrolux is one of the world leaders in household appliances and vacuum cleaners, Volvo is amongst the five largest manufacturers of relatively exclusive automobiles and second in heavy trucks, Sandvik has a leading position in rock drills, and so on.

Industry Status

The emphasis in the activities of Swedish multinationals abroad is different, in industry terms, when compared with Swedish domestic manufacturing. Thus the engineering industry represents 75 per cent of foreign operations but only 46 per cent of industrial employment in Sweden. On the other hand, mining, ferrous and non-ferrous metal production and the forestry industry, where proximity to the source of raw materials is important, have relatively limited operations abroad. Swedish companies, in contrast with their American equivalents, have not gone into business overseas to exploit foreign raw materials. Swedish industry has been more interested in locating certain manufacturing operations, in the later stages of the production process, close to the market. As already mentioned, the clothing industry is unique in setting up manufacturing operations based on local resources.

Table 3.4: Distribution by Industry of Employees and Assets in Manufacturing Subsidiaries in 1960, 1970, 1974 and 1978

Industry	Employees (%)				Assets (%)			
	1960	1970	1974	1978	1960	1970	1974	1978
Food	} 0.5	1	1	} 1	} 0.7	1	1	} 1
Textile and Clothing		2	3	2		1	1	0
Pulp and Paper		2	2	4		7	6	6
Paper products and printing		2	3	6		3	4	5
Chemicals	21	14	11	8	14	8	8	7
Metals and metal goods	7	10	12	12	11	14	13	14
Machinery	47	43	33	34	50	43	32	37
Electrical goods	19	18	24	21	18	15	22	15
Transportation goods	1	2	5	8	1	3	7	11
Other industries	5	6	6	4	5	5	6	4
All industries	100	100	100	100	100	100	100	100

Source: SOU (1982:27)

The status of the various industries operating abroad has changed somewhat since 1960 (see Table 3.4). Industries previously involved in foreign production (i.e. the chemicals and machinery industries) have declined in importance while the paper/pulp and transport equipment industries have increased their shares. The electrical/electronics industry has expanded, with the exception of the most recent period where a decline was the result of Ericsson's forced sale of a major subsidiary to local interests.

Increased International Dependence

The companies' dependence on international dealings can be estimated either in terms of foreign sales, expressed as a percentage of total sales, or as the proportion of production carried out abroad. As Figure 3.3 indicates, both these proportions have increased between 1965 and 1978.

Figure 3.3: The Swedish Multinationals: Percentage of Sales and Production at Home and Abroad, 1965, 1970, 1974 and 1978

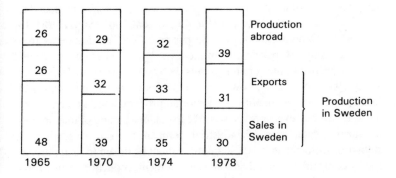

Source: SOU (1982:27)

The most obvious factor is that foreign sales have increased from 52 per cent to 70 per cent of total sales. The twenty largest multinationals now achieve three-quarters of their sales abroad (Table 3.5).

If we turn to manufacturing abroad, we find that exports comprised half of foreign sales in 1965 — the other half consisting of manufacturing

Table 3.5: Foreign Sales in Relation to Total Sales of the 20 Largest Swedish Multinational Corporations, 1978–83

	1978	1979	1980	1981	1982	1983
%	69	70	68	71	74	76

Source: Annual reports.

abroad. Total foreign sales abroad grew until 1974, but the proportions attributable to exports and foreign manufacturing remained roughly constant — manufacturing in Sweden destined for export expanded at the same rate as foreign manufacturing. After 1974, however, foreign production increased twice as rapidly as exports, with the result that the share of foreign sales represented by foreign manufacturing increased to 56 per cent. The centre of gravity in multinational companies has thus shifted abroad, since both foreign sales and foreign manufacturing have become relatively more significant while sales and production in Sweden have become less important.

The significance of foreign subcontractors is an additional aspect of the international dependence of Swedish multinationals. It is, however, difficult to measure this factor. Figures obtained from Volvo indicate that 70 per cent of the parts and components used in automobile manufacturing originate abroad compared to 45 per cent 1967 (SOU, 1981:43. pp. 350 ff). Volvo now buys in 35 per cent of its requirements from West Germany, 10 per cent from the UK, 7 per cent from France and 18 per cent from other countries outside Sweden (*Svenska Dagbladet*, 9 July 1984). Normally, however, companies are not able to supply information as to the quantities of imported products used in their operations. It has, however, proved possible to obtain a picture of total imports of various categories of industrial companies from Swedish trade statistics. Unfortunately, these figures cannot be linked to total purchasing by companies, but only to the value of their production. Some reservations must be made about the accuracy of the figures, since companies may pursue reselling operations in varying degrees. In so far as we can rely on these statistics, however, we find that the proportion of imports in production was 19 per cent for Swedish multinationals, 11 per cent for other Swedish industrial companies and 30 per cent for foreign-owned companies. Differences between Swedish multinationals and national companies were apparent in all industries, except wood products and chemicals.

Despite proportional increases in both foreign production and foreign sales over time, it does not appear that individual companies are more interested in foreign manufacturing if they have a high proportion of foreign sales. Table 3.6 indicates that there is no consistent link between the proportion of foreign sales and the proportion of foreign production. Only multinational companies with more than 80 per cent of their sales abroad have a significantly higher proportion of their production located outside Sweden than other companies.

Table 3.6: Foreign Production as Proportion of Foreign Sales in 1970 and 1978, for groups of companies classified by proportion of turnover sold abroad

Foreign sales as percentage of total group turnover	1970		1978	
	No. of groups	Foreign production as percentage of foreign sales	No. of groups	Foreign production as percentage of foreign sales
0 – 20	14	39	9	49
21 – 40	24	33	19	46
41 – 60	31	35	28	43
61 – 80	24	36	40	49
81 –100	12	60	14	63
Total	105	42	110	52

Source: SOU (1982:27) and Swedenborg (1973).

Figures describing the number of employees in the 20 largest multinationals from 1979 to 1983 indicate that these companies expanded less, or rationalised more intensively, than in the 1960s and 1970s. In fact, the number of employees working for the major multinationals has increased very little, either in Sweden or abroad, in the last five years (see Figure 3.4). Indeed, over the last two years there has been a reduction in the size of the labour force, both in Sweden and in foreign subsidiaries. SKF has reduced the numbers employed abroad by approximately 6,000, while Ericsson has made cuts of 500 personnel in Mexico alone, following the phasing out of electromechanical telephone exchanges and the introduction of electronic equipment. These figures may perhaps indicate that rationalisation and restructuring processes in mature multinational companies affect foreign operations at least as much as domestic.

Figure 3.4: Changes in Number of Employees in Sweden and Abroad in the 20 Largest Swedish Multinationals, 1979-83*

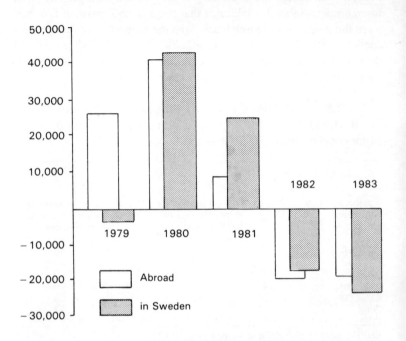

* The companies are listed in Appendix A.
Source: Company annual reports

Various Ways of Setting Up Foreign Operations

There is a rather natural tendency automatically to associate the direct investment concept with the setting-up of new manufacturing facilities. i.e. the building of new factories. In point of fact, however, a large and increasing proportion of direct investments abroad involve the acquisition of existing companies (see Table 3.7). In the 1960s, acquisitions represented less than 40 per cent of investments abroad, but this proportion increased to over 60 per cent in the 1970s. There may be several explanations for this change — for example there was a generally poor market growth in the 1970s and multinational companies could expand more cheaply by buying up market shares from their competitors.

Table 3.7: Swedish Foreign Direct Investments, 1966–78,
by type of establishment

Type of Establishment	No. of Manufacturing Subsidiaries Established	
	1960–1970	1971–1978
Greenfield investments	105	54
Previously sales companies	50	50
Acquired	99	163
Total	254	267

Source: SOU (1982:27).

Forsgren and Larsson (1984) have studied appoximately 280 acquisitions, involving the 50 largest Swedish multinationals and covering the
period 1970–82. They found that 32 per cent of acquisitions involved
the purchase of a competitor, as when Sandvik, which already had a
French subsidiary, purchased the French company, Le Burin. Sandvik's
intention was certainly to increase its market share in France, but it was
perhaps even more important to hinder other companies from increasing their market share. In 34 per cent of the acquisition cases studied,
the company making the purchase, while active in the same field of operations as the company acquired, was not represented on the local market.
Here the reason for acquisitions was market expansion. An example here
might be the purchase of National Union Electric by Electrolux in order
to enter the American vacuum cleaner market. Previously Electrolux
had not sold vacuum cleaners in the United States, since the Electrolux
'trade mark' was owned by another company.

Forsgren and Larsson found that it was less common (10 per cent
of cases) for the company acquired to be involved in operations which
were similar to those of the buyer, but yet not directly competitive. In
such cases, acquisition was a way of broadening the product range rapidly
and gaining further know-how. Thus Atlas Copco, which manufactures
rock drilling equipment, purchased the American Jarva Inc., which
specialised in drilling equipment for soft geological formations. A similar
number of acquisitions (9 per cent) involved increased vertical integration. An example here is when ASSI, a manufacturer of the paper used
for sacking, purchased a British paper sack maker, Flexer Paper Sacks.
The remaining 15 per cent of company purchases were characterised

as conglomerate acquisitions, which indicates that there was no link either with the Swedish company's technology or its customers. Most of the companies purchased were small. One of the larger examples was the American Dymo company, a manufacturer of marking equipment. The purchaser was Esselte, whose main field of operations involved publishing and printing.

The status of foreign subsidiaries in the multinational group is likely to differ, at least initially, depending on whether they are new creations or the result of the acquisition of existing companies. Table 3.8 serves to illustrate this to some extent. The acquired subsidiaries purchase relatively less from Sweden and they purchase different types of products. As might be expected, former sales companies are the heaviest

Table 3.8: Foreign Manufacturing Subsidiaries Established in 1971–8 — numbers, assets, employees, exports and imports in 1978, by method of establishment

	All Subsidiaries 1978	Distribution (%)			
		Greenfield Investments	Former Sales Subsidiaries	Acquisitions	Total
No. of subsidiaries	249	20	19	61	100
No. of employees	63,151	9	14	77	100
Total assets (Skr million)	6,122	9	17	74	100
Volume of capital transferred from Sweden (Skr million)	1,671	7	15	78	100
Turnover (Skr million)	6,388	8	16	76	100
Imports from Swedish group companies (Skr million)	1,255	10	41	49	100
of which:					
Finished goods	621	7	63	30	100
Components	617	14	22	64	100
Investment goods	17	55	9	36	100
Exports (Skr million)	1,285	11	6	83	100
of which:					
Exports to Sweden	216	22	11	67	100

Source: SOU (1982:27).

purchasers from the parent company. Newly established subsidiaries are also more involved in supplying their local market, while acquisitions may have a long tradition as exporters.

Financing and Ownership

Company direct investments abroad do not primarily reflect differences in the return on capital by different countries and this is confirmed by the fact that investments flow in both directions across frontiers. Information released by the American Department of Trade for 1975 indicates, furthermore, that American companies' foreign investments were only partially financed in the United States. A similar situation applies for Swedish multinationals' foreign investments (see Table 3.9). The Central Bank of Sweden has required (since 1976) that direct investments abroad must be financed abroad, if the investment does not involve a purely sales-oriented company or some other special case.

Table 3.9: Permits for Outward Direct Investment, by method of transaction (%)

	1974	1978	1981	1982	1983
Transfer from Sweden	27	17	15	21	17
Financed abroad	59	56	77	68	78
Other	14	27	8	11	5
	100	100	100	100	100

Source: The Central Bank of Sweden

The fact that companies are not permitted to transfer capital outside Sweden, combined with stagnation of sales in Sweden and the resultant low level of investments, has led to the accumulation of cash mountains of liquid reserves in the Swedish units belonging to multinational groups. The unilateral loan financing of foreign investments has led to a deterioration in solvency ratings. As a corrective measure, some Swedish multinationals have started to launch new share issues abroad. As indicated in Table 3.10, export permits for Swedish shares have increased considerably, amounting, in 1983, to a somewhat larger sum than permits for outward direct investment.

Share emissions have mainly involved institutional buyers in Great Britain and the United States. The proportion of the equity of certain

Table 3.10: Exports and Imports of Shares of Swedish
Corporations, 1981–3 (Skr million)

Year	Exports	Of which placing new shares	Imports
1981	1,461	303	1,120
1982	2,704	128	1,335
1983	11,951	3,904	5,840
1984	5,958	371	4,471

Source: The Central Bank of Sweden

companies held by foreign interests has increased considerably in a remarkably short time. Foreigners — mainly Americans — now own 38 per cent of Ericsson shares. However, at present these shares carry reduced voting rights. Another important reason for the increase in the sale of shares abroad is that it creates favourable publicity which can help sales. If a Swedish company's shares are quoted on a foreign stock market, it is also easier to purchase foreign companies and pay for such acquisitions by means of shares in the Swedish company.

4 THEORIES OF FOREIGN DIRECT INVESTMENT

In 1897, AB Separator (now Alfa-Laval) purchased a small factory in Vienna for the manufacture of dairy equipment, designed to supplement the company's patented main product, the separator, which was exported from Sweden (Wohlert, 1981, p. 168). In 1983 the Swedish penicillin manufacturer, Fermenta, purchased a penicillin plant in France. The present main shareholder and managing director of Fermenta originally came from Egypt and the French factory was sold by an American pharmaceutical corporation. These examples imply that direct foreign investments by companies are both heterogeneous and changing phenomena. This presents considerable problems to anyone attempting to explain the phenomenon of direct investments. Inevitably, a general theory will have very little information value. Relatively precise predictions can only be made if we confine ourselves to explaining certain types of direct investment, or the investments of certain companies. This chapter attempts to summarise the theoretical basis for the studies which we have undertaken and, to some extent, to comment on the theories on the basis of the experience we have gained in studying foreign investments by Swedish companies.

Hymer's doctoral thesis (1960) can be said to be the basis for the modern understanding of the origin of foreign direct investments. Foreign investments by companies had previously been chiefly regarded as movements of capital which could be explained in terms of differences in capital yields in various countries. Hymer tried, instead, to explain the behaviour of companies investing abroad in terms of industrial organisation theory. This approach was later supplemented by explanations originating in localisation theory and the theory of property rights — Dunning coined the expression 'eclectic theory' to explain foreign direct investments.

In the 1970s there was growing discussion of the possibilities of adding to eclectic theory and later also replacing eclectic theory by a more general theory based on corporate growth (internalisation theory). The central point in internalisation theory involves a comparison of the alternatives of coordinating economic activities (i) through the market mechanism, (ii) through a hierarchy. Theoretical discussion at this level can be extremely interesting, although sometimes it becomes somewhat confused due to varying concepts and assumptions applied by various authors. In our view, there is a difference between eclectic theory and internalisation theory and we will comment more on this difference at a later stage. We have chosen to take the eclectic theory as our starting point and then to discuss internalisation as an extension of the eclectic approach.

The Eclectic Theory

A special characteristic of eclectic theory is, as implied by the name, that it consists of several theories which each, individually, explain certain aspects of the phenomenon under study. Although direct investments are the point of the exercise, increasing attention is paid to flows of know-how and goods and to the control of production activities. The questions dealt with by eclectic theory are, firstly, how a company manages to survive and maintain its position in a foreign market; secondly, why companies prefer to manufacture products abroad rather than enter into licensing agreements or exporting; thirdly, why direct investments occur in some countries but not in others.

How Can Some Companies Succeed in Staying Competitive in Foreign Markets?

Hymer started with the assumption that a company which establishes itself in another country faces considerable difficulties which would not be encountered by a domestic company. It should, for example, be easier to conduct commercial operations in the home country where customers, suppliers, laws and business practices are all known. The foreign company should therefore, at least initially, be faced by higher costs than the corresponding domestic company. If the foreign company is to vindicate itself, it must have advantages or superiority in some respects which more than compensate for the disadvantage of being a foreigner. If it proves possible to define and specify such competitive advantages, we have arrived at an important explanation of the phenomenon of direct investments.

Hymer's thesis was that companies which undertake, or can undertake, direct investments have competitive advantages similar to those which characterise established companies in oligopoly situations (i.e. a product market dominated by a few companies). Competitive advantages may be the result of the manufacturing method employed, or may be linked to the marketing function. A company may have created the impression, by various means, that their products are different or better than those of their competitors. This does not necessarily mean that the products cannot be substituted but simply that they have some characteristics which differentiate them from others. This implies that the product is sold under its own trade name and normally through its own sales organisation. Whatever the reason for the competitive advantages, they must result in situations where the products can be sold at higher than cost price plus 'normal business profit', or otherwise there is, by definition, no competitive advantage.

Studies of industries in which Swedish multinational companies are active indicate that the essential competitive advantages may change over time. A company may establish new advantages, resulting from exploitation of the original advantages, and we may thus speak of an 'advantages cycle' (Sandén and Vahlne, 1976). The original advantage of Swedish multinational companies in foreign markets consisted of technological know-how which enabled them to produce products which were competitive on an international scale. In order to sell these products in foreign markets, the companies built up international sales organisations. This meant that Swedish multinationals acquired an increasingly broad experience of foreign markets and marketing, as time went by, which included confidential and long-term relationships with customers. Increased marketing experience and links with customers became, in turn, a competitive advantage which became of increasing importance as the significance of technological superiority declined. At a later stage in the process, new competitive advantages occurred which might be characterised as 'multinational advantages'. These advantages are the result of superior information systems and knowledge of markets possessed by multinational companies, improving their decision-making capacity as regards, for example, manufacturing inputs and marketing activities and enabling them to allocate their resources in a more efficient manner than other companies.

Studies of the internationalisation process experienced by Swedish companies have also indicated that the *need* for competitive advantages can change over time. From the theoretical point of view, competitive advantages are necessary to counteract the handicaps which face foreign companies. One expression of such handicaps might be the 'psychological' distance between various countries. In a previous study, we tried to operationalise such distances, indicating the number of variables such as language, differences in business practices and standards of living (Hörnell and Vahlne, 1972). Empirical studies then showed, amongst other things, that exports and foreign investments went first to 'culturally' close countries but that, as time went on, and the company had established itself in a number of countries, it was no longer possible to trace any clear correlation between choice of market and the 'cultural' closeness. Furthermore, it could be noted that the companies were more likely to establish their own sales organisations in a new export country directly, instead of engaging a local representative, if they had previously had subsidiaries in several countries. These results indicate that the 'cultural' distance is most critical in the case of initial establishment abroad in a limited number of countries, but that companies subsequently acquire knowledge and experience of doing business in other countries which is more generally applicable. As a result, the handicap factor becomes less important and thus the need for competitive advantages is reduced.

Quite apart from our reservations as regards the need for competitive advantages, we find that the existence of competitive advantages is not sufficient reason for a company to establish manufacturing operations in another country. The company could, instead, export goods abroad or transfer the manufacturing rights to local companies in exchange for some financial compensation. What we have to explain, therefore, is why companies choose to conduct manufacturing operations in their own name.

Why Do Companies Exploit their Advantages Within their Own Organisations?

When a company has a competitive advantage based upon patent or trademark rights, it is usually possible to exploit this advantage in a foreign market by licensing such rights to a local company. There are, however, several problems and risks involved from the licenser's point of view. One argument against licensing a product to a foreign company is the potential threat of the licensee ultimately becoming a competitor. Such a situation might, in fact, occur if the licensee acquires sufficient know-how as a result of the licensing agreement so that he could develop similar products himself. The foreign company may also eventually become a competitor when the patent or license period expires. A further explanation of the reluctance to transfer the exploitation of unique competitive assets to a licensee is that continuous 'maintenance work' is required. Maintenance of market position is often dependent on constant product development and improvements in sales methods. The licenser may find it difficult to control the licensee's operations in these respects.

It is even more difficult and more risky to sell a competitive advantage which is not based on patent or trade-mark rights. Certain kinds of know-how are practically impossible to sell. They can only be exploited within the company of origin. In such cases the alternative to licensing is primarily to manufacture the product in the company's own plant and then export it. The solution which would then comply best with the 'free competition model' would be to select a suitable foreign representative as an intermediary. Unfortunately, the arguments which we have used previously to indicate the potential risks in licensing also apply in the case of exports via foreign agents. Our previous studies of the establishment of facilities abroad indicated that the propensity to export via wholly-owned sales companies was greatest for companies with 'high technology' products. Such products have a high software weighting which creates problems when establishing prices and such products require a smooth information flow between the manufacturer and the market. Establishing a sales subsidiary also reduces the company's difficulties in distributing costs and revenues on a fair basis between the manufacturing operation and the foreign sales organisation.

When we turn to the question of why foreign manufacturing is preferred to the alternative of exporting via sales companies, we should first note that foreign manufacturing by Swedish multinational companies is, in many cases, the result of a further development of a sales subsidiary. Such sales subsidiaries started by undertaking certain manufacturing processes which occurred in the final stages of production (e.g., assembly or adaptation to local market requirements). Subsequently the subsidiaries' operations were extended to cover the entire manufacturing process, although, generally speaking, this did not include some key aspects of production. To some extent, the reason for undertaking local manufacturing was the result of cost advantages (e.g., lower transport costs), but sales advantages were probably a more important factor. Customers could have products modified to meet their own requirements more readily and in many cases local manufacturing was essential, especially if the customer was in the public sector.

Internalisation theory offers a more general explanation of why companies exploit competitive advantages within their own organisations. Internalisation theory takes as its starting point the idea that economic activities can either be coordinated amongst independent companies in a market, or within one company under central management. The question is seen from the point of view of a company investing abroad and the question is whether it is more profitable to control foreign production within one organisation or company group or to sell know-how and products via independent companies. Here we find two reasons which tend to make the hierarchical solution more profitable. One reason is that it is risky and expensive to rely on the market in certain situations. This is identical with the line of argument which we have already encountered regarding the problems of licensing and exporting via local agents. Another point in favour of the hierarchical solution is that co-ordination within an organisation can in itself achieve advantages. There may be advantages of scale of the multiplant type, there may be coordination gains or synergy effects and, finally, integration may well reduce competition, thus giving the organisation or company group monopolistic yields and returns.

Internalisation theory can be said to be a more general description of why it may prove advantageous for companies to grow, irrespective of whether such growth takes place within one country or across national frontiers. This extension of the theory is reasonable, especially in the light of our belief that national frontiers have become less important and that it has become more significant to regard the object under study as a large company with international sales. Rugman (1983) asserted that the substantial difference between the eclectic theory and the internalisation theory is the assumption that market imperfections are endogenous or exogenous. An example in favour of the line that market imperfections are exogenous is that a multinational group of companies is likely to pay lower taxes and tariff duties as a result of internal pricing than two independent companies. However, this incentive is probably of somewhat marginal significance. We consider that a better example would be direct investments in the form of company acquisitions, where the intention is to acquire new know-how or new products which, in combination with the existing range, can provide a higher yield than would have been possible with two independent companies. Although we think that the company's specific advantages are not necessary to justify direct investment, we believe that the presence of an advantage increases the probability that the hierarchical solution, through a foreign direct investment, will prove the most profitable from the company point of view.

Which Countries Receive Direct Investment?

We have already mentioned that the typical pattern for Swedish companies has been that export sales, and also the establishment of sales subsidiaries, have initially taken place in countries which are both geographically and 'culturally' close. However, foreign production has not always occurred first in the very closest countries and the question is how the distribution of foreign direct investments amongst various countries can be explained. Discussion of the company-specific advantages gives no real indication of where foreign production is likely to be carried out. The theory of foreign direct investments must therefore be strengthened by explanations as to why companies decide to progress beyond exports, via sales subsidiaries, in certain countries.

Hirsch (1976) has done considerable research which attempts to explain the influences on company attitudes of direct investments in various countries. Hirsch has analysed the company's choice between locating the production in the domestic market or in a given foreign market by studying factors such as production costs in the relevant countries, export costs and the costs of controlling a foreign subsidiary. In Sweden, Swedenborg (1979) has found that the factors which above all favour foreign production rather than exports are trade barriers, manufacturing costs in the relevant countries and the scale of plant installations in the industry involved. The scale factor thus means that a certain market size is required if local production is to be viable. Trade barriers, combined with manufacturing costs on the local market, are then decisive in the question of whether production is cheaper or not. The result is that companies prefer to manufacture in countries with large markets, high trade barriers and low manufacturing costs while preferring to export to small countries with low trade barriers and high manufacturing costs.

The explanations of the dispersion of direct investments by country given so far have been on an industry level, since the scale of plant assets and trade barriers and manufacturing costs must necessarily be discussed on the basis of a given industry. On the same description level, the same line of argumentation can also be used within the framework of internalisation theory. If we decide, instead, to regard internalisation theory as a general theory which explains all direct investments, the question then becomes whether there are systematic differences between different countries with regard to how well markets or hierarchies function. Hennart (1982) has used this method to explain differences between various countries as regards the *outflow* of direct investments. The USA's previously large share of world direct investments, seen in relative terms, might then be explained by superiority in respect of management know-how, which means that the hierarchical solution proved more profitable for American companies. It would then be possible to explain, along similar lines, the relatively limited direct investments from Japan by suggesting that there have been better conditions in Japan for achieving coordination using non-hierarchical solutions. Such conditions, operating in the Japanese case, might be based on a different cultural pattern which, amongst other things, reduces the risks of utilising the market.

Concluding Remarks

It is obvious that companies invest abroad because they consider such investment as being the most profitable solution. The most interesting theoretical question is therefore why, or under what conditions, foreign investments appear to be the most profitable. An essential factor in this connection is that companies wish to exploit know-how or some other intangible asset. Such assets may be seen first as an opportunity to go out to a foreign market and, later, also as a reason for conducting manufacturing activities in several countries within the framework of a company group or organisation. The eclectic theory can be said to be most relevant for the early stages in the internationalisation processes when national frontiers represent real barriers. In later stages, as the company grows internationally, it seems to be reasonable to de-emphasise the crossing of national frontiers and to stress more the growth and steering aspects within the framework of internalisation theory.

5 A MODEL FOR AN INDUSTRIAL CHANGE PROCESS

Although many of the explanations of the origin of multinational companies are based on conditions at a company level, empirical research has placed greater emphasis on characteristics at an industry level (Caves, 1971; Horst, 1973). This does not necessarily imply any inconsistency: the characteristics of individual companies may be said to reflect the characteristics of the industries within which they operate. However, tendencies in the casual relations can be discussed. Characteristics at the industry level are, of course, the result of exogenous conditions to some extent, but also reflect the attempts of companies to change certain industry characteristics to suit their own requirements. This constitutes, or should constitute, the real meaning of much that is implied by the term 'strategic management' (Porter, 1980). Other companies must adjust to such changes in order to survive in a competitive world.

As we have already indicated, we have preferred to regard the internationalisation of companies as a process — or rather as an element of a continuous process. Internationalisation at the company level has its equivalent at the industry level — not only in the sense that competition becomes internationalised, but also in that different types of changes occur. The aim, in this chapter, is to develop a model to describe changes at the industry level which appear to form the basis of companies' internationalisation process. In this context, we define an industry as a group of companies which are competing with each other in the solving of problems to meet the specific requirements of a specific group of customers. It is not easy to present an unambiguous and clear theoretical definition of this group of companies, but in practice the companies themselves can none the less list their competitors.

As already indicated in previous chapters, the engineering industry plays a dominant role in the foreign activities of Swedish industry, and most of the major Swedish multinational companies operate in the engineering industry. The model which follows is based on observations made in five sectors in the engineering industry which typify the situation of Swedish multinational companies (see Table 5.1). At a later stage, we will describe the development process in the clothing industry and it will then become apparent that the validity of our model is limited to the engineering industry.

Table 5.1: Sectors of the Engineering Industries Studied and Swedish Multinational Companies Operating in these Sectors

Welding equipment	AGA, ESAB
Cemented carbide rock drills	Fagersta, Sandvik
Rock-drill equipment	Atlas Copco
Ventilation equipment	Bacho, Fläkt
Telecommunications equipment	Ericsson

The origin of the model can be traced to observations of regular trends and patterns in the companies which have been studied and in the development of the sectors in which they operate. Armed with theoretical frameworks acquired primarily in areas such as industrial organisation and the eclectic theory of the multinational corporations, our aim was to describe and analyse the development of companies in respect of the effects of direct investments made by these companies. We studied published material about these industrial sectors and the companies in question and interviewed representatives of the companies, customers and competitors. When comparing results, it appeared that developments in the various companies and industries displayed certain similar — if not identical — characteristics. These characteristics are presented in Table 5.2 which gives a summarised picture of the model.

Table 5.2: A Model for the Change Process in an Industrial Sector

Characteristics	Phase 1	Phase 2	Phase 3
Type of competition	Monopolistic	Increased concentration	Oligopolistic
Geographic spread	Local	Regional	Global
What was sold?	Products	Subsystems	Systems
Form of supply to market	Export agents	Export-sales subsidiaries	Local manufacturing International sourcing
Competitive tools	Price Quality	Marketing Service	Solve customers' problems
Company specific advantages	Technology Raw materials	Relations to customers	Ability to develop new technology 'Size'
Type of growth	Internal expansion in Sweden	Establishment of foreign subsidiaries	Acquisition (Cooperation)

The development of companies and of industries is, of course, a continuous process. In the interests of clarity, this process has been subdivided into three consecutive phases which we consider to be relevant. There is also a fourth phase — but this is discussed later. The phases of the different sectors are not strictly parallel in terms of time, since different technologies develop and change at different rates. The ventilation industry did not take off until well into the twentieth century whereas steel has been manufactured for more than a century. The phases are also of varying duration for various industries. The ventilation industry is not yet involved in global competition but none the less shows some signs of the characteristics which apply to the global competition phase.[1] We shall discuss the possible reasons at a later stage.

The duration of the various phases appears to become increasingly brief the closer we come to the present day, due to the rate of technological development.

The Model

The companies studied have acquired technological know-how, which became a company-specific advantage, either when they were founded or at a very early stage in their development. This know-how or knowledge was either based on an invention, as in the case of Ericsson or, as in the case of Sandvik, from the acquisition of the right to manufacture steel using the Bessemer method. The company-specific advantages were exploited by manufacturing and selling products based on the new technology. In direct contrast with other types of assets, the value of such know-how and technological knowledge is not reduced by being exploited on a large scale. It is therefore normally profitable to expand by selling a company product on new — usually foreign — markets. This is, in fact, the case in the companies that have been studied.

In the early stages of the companies' history what was being sold could be characterised as 'products' — telephones or railway carriage wheels. Customers acquired the products and used them in the production process. The selling process, which in the early stages was often transacted by agents, consisted in many cases simply of taking orders or presenting straightforward arguments about price and quality. It was a question of selling the factory output.

The value of the company-specific advantages led to a financial surplus — not surprisingly, since we have studied successful companies.

Broadly speaking, surplus may be said to have been used in two different ways: in product development which led to a superior and broader product range, and in the establishment and expansion of a network of subsidiaries with a marketing and storage function. As time passed, Ericsson began to manufacture not only telephones, but also telephone exchanges, cable and other products needed for a total tele-communications system. Sandvik, on the other hand, successfully replaced its agents, especially in the 1920s and 1930s, by wholly-owned sales subsidiaries.

Wholly-owned sales organisations were not only superior in attaining good sales results but were also to prove valuable intermediaries in the transfer of information from customers back to the management functions responsible for product development and the product range. Close relationships and situations involving mutual dependencies were often built up between the Swedish company and its representatives, on the one hand, and the purchasing company and its staff on the other. As a result, there was often a long-term link between the seller and the buyer. This made it more difficult for competitors to win over the Swedish company's buyers.

Other important results were that the employees of the sales subsidiaries came to understand the buyer's production process and were fully acquainted with how the Swedish company's products fitted into this production process. Against this background of inside information, the parent company was able to develop product systems which were exactly tailored to the buyer's requirements. Probably, in some cases, the sales subsidiaries became more competent than the buyers in their knowledge of the purchasing companies' production processes.

It is likely that the Swedish manufacturers did not have any permanent technological superiority, since the rate of technological development has sometimes slowed down, and some competitors have been able to imitate Swedish products successfully. Instead, ties with the buyers and the established marketing and service networks have been the Swedish companies' primary advantages. In accordance with the previously mentioned model of cyclical advantages (Chapter 4), the exploitation of the original advantage has lead to the establishment of new or additional advantages.

Companies which have proved unable to maintain the value of the company-specific advantage or to develop new advantages have tended to cease to function as independent companies, either because they have been acquired by competitors or because they have gone into liquidation. As a result, the degree of concentration increased.

Improved information about the buyers' production processes and the role played by the Swedish companies' own products in these processes was increasingly exploited — for example, Swedish manufacturers began to supply more or less complete solutions to the buyers' problems. Such systems tend to be based on the company's own products, but sometimes also other companies' products, combined in such a manner that they might cover the buyer's entire production process — in extreme cases. An important, if not the most important, part in such a system lies in knowledge of how the various products, and modifications of these products, should be combined, how the system should be operated and how its operating reliability can be maintained. Thus, companies in the telecommunications business have been capable of supplying complete systems for many decades. This is reflected in the design of the Ericsson subsidiaries which were organised and staffed in such a way that, in extreme cases, each manager in the telecommunications administration which purchased the companies' products could contact a certain subsidiary employee capable of solving any specific problem that might arise. Another example is the combination of Sandvik drills and Atlas Copco drilling equipment which became accepted as a rock-drilling system in the 1950s — clearly with considerable success.

A move towards increasingly complex and differentiated products has taken place, while the number of competitors has simultaneously declined and the size of the remaining companies has increased. The companies left in the game have had to attain a minimum size in order to achieve the necessary level of investments in research and development and marketing organisations.

In the ventilation and welding sectors, there are a greater number of competitors than is the case in telecommunications and drilling equipment. It is not a pleasant situation for an individual company to belong to an industry characterised by monopolistic competition with many competitors and keen price competition. This type of competitive situation inevitably means that it is difficult to generate a financial surplus. Individual companies will therefore attempt to extricate themselves from this type of situation. Extrication may well involve the acquisition of competitors, and this may therefore be an expression of a conscious attempt to 'improve' the company's competitive situation. The interesting point in this context is that the establishment of marketing, contracting and service activities, together with research and development, also form valuable competitive barriers for companies which are unable to make corresponding investments — this is the case both in Sweden and foreign markets. The building up of marketing networks and the resultant creation of stable relationships with customers and changes in products and systems is a slow process. The original intention is probably not to change the market structure of the industry — but modifications are an inevitable result.

Development in the welding and ventilation sectors may be seen against this background. The contracting operations of Bacho and Fläkt and the resultant development of system products constitute today (and will probably also constitute in the future) company-specific advantages which change the competitive situation. We may well ask why this development process has been relatively slower in the welding and ventilation industries than has been the case with rock drills and (even more) telecommunications. The probable answer lies in varying requirements placed on the products and systems involved.

Telecommunications requirements are solved by the establishment of a unified telephone system for a given country. This means that the number of buyers is heavily restricted — normally only one buyer for each country. Requirements in the welding and ventilation industries, on the other hand, vary much more — climatic factors and the characteristics of metals or of buildings are involved, for example. It has therefore proved difficult to design systems with broad areas of application, as has been possible in telecommunications. This is also a major reason why the number of installation contractors is so large in the ventilation industry.

When the work on the design of systems to meet specific requirements commences, it is likely that the number of manufacturers will be reduced. Furthermore, it is probably true that companies which are vertically integrated in a forward direction are better placed to grasp and understand the potential for improvements in the product range. Manufacturing companies only interested in disposing of their products will inevitably lose ground.

Some companies have, however, specialised in the manufacture of a very limited number of products — in extreme cases only one product or even only one component. There are, for example, companies which specialise in the production of inlet and exhaust valves. Although there may, of course, be many models and variations of such components in the manufacturer's full range, the central feature of such activities lies in the opportunities to cut costs by means of highly mechanised, large-scale production processes.

In all the engineering sectors that we have studied, we have noted a tendency for system manufacturers to attempt to standardise at the product level — and this is even truer at the component level. This has led to a situation where a single product or component manufacturer may supply several systems manufacturers. To an increasing extent, the results seem to have been that the systems manufacturers have stopped making certain components themselves — especially the simple types.

We have not studied the factors which affect costs in the component manufacturing stages, but we consider it very likely that the length of the production run is of great importance in this context. If this proposition is true, it might explain why so many components are supplied by manufacturers in major countries, such as West Germany. Companies in such countries have probably attained a lead as regards manufacturing capacity which Swedish component manufacturers will find it difficult to catch up. The implications of our study, therefore, tend to support the view that Sweden is well on the way to becoming 'an assembly plant'.

It has already been pointed out that a number of companies in the ventilation and welding sectors have chosen to specialise, employing low manufacturing costs as a competitive weapon. We should, however, also pay attention to another dimension of specialisation. The greater part of sales volume still consists of products, rather than systems. Since well-established relationships with users are important, we would expect to find a number of companies specialising in a certain region. This presents advantages in terms of proximity to buyers. But if systems solutions become increasingly acceptable, the value of this advantage is reduced and regionally specialised companies can become interesting take-over propositions for systems manufacturers.

Generally speaking, Swedish engineering companies' initial investments abroad have been in marketing and distribution networks. The advantages created by these networks, combined with advantages of a technological nature, have made it possible to go on to establish manufacturing facilities abroad, where this has been considered justified. The alternative of manufacturing locally has often been seen as superior from the company point of view, since the local market was protected by trade barriers. In the case of the establishment of manufacturing operations in Western Europe, most Swedish companies set up their production facilities well before the creation of duty-free areas. In the case of other regions, tariff barriers are still an important factor. Furthermore, in many countries there are also non-tariff barriers to be considered. A further reason for setting up local manufacturing facilities has been that the buyers have preferred, or demanded, locally manufactured products, as in the case of telecommunications. Transport costs have also made direct exports from Sweden impossible, as has been the case with certain bulky ventilation products. To express the situation in another way: the value of the package of advantages has not been sufficient to outweigh the disadvantage of exporting from Sweden — but the advantages have been sufficient to permit local manufacturing.

Local manufacturing has also developed on a stage-by-stage basis. Generally speaking, it is the final phases in the production process in the relevant market which most have been affected.[2] The final stage of manufacturing has typically involved product adaptation or assembly. Exports to Sweden or the third countries have been relatively unusual at this stage. There has been no exploitation of possible country-specific advantages in host countries. If there have been lower costs for labour, these have normally been accompanied by lower productivity. Instead, it has been a question of purely 'market' investments in the production operation, sometimes in parallel with investments made in Sweden.

The object of establishing local manufacturing has been to increase sales. In the long-term perspective, it was even more important that the companies making such investments improved their product-adaptation capacity, and hence became involved in more, and closer, relationships with customers. From this point of view, local production can be viewed as a stage in the marketing process.

Another typical characteristic of this phase in the internationalisation process has been that investments have taken place in the form of greenfields establishments of manufacturing facilities. Less frequently, acquisition of existing companies has been involved. The investments have meant an advance of competitive positions. The 'foreignness' of the company, with all its associated disadvantages, has been reduced. Some of the weaker domestic competitors have been eliminated. We may say that oligopoly undoubtedly creates a situation favourable to direct investments and international companies, but that direct investments are, in their turn, a stage in a continued oligopolisation process. Ultimately, the result is the establishment of global oligopolies.

It is clear from previous chapters that the various engineering industry sectors have made varying progress in the concentration process which runs parallel with technological development and internationalisation. Telecommunications have been heavily concentrated for many years. The rock-drill equipment sector, on the other hand, has achieved a high degree of concentration relatively recently. The welding and ventilation sectors still have a relatively low level of concentration, but, as has already been discussed, there is reason to believe that the degree of concentration will increase in the future.

Thus, a discussion of competitive behaviour in a global oligopoly may take the telecommunications and rock-drill sectors as a starting point. In these industries, the number of competitors is restricted. Barriers to establishment for companies outside the industry have become extremely difficult to overcome. All the competitors may participate, in principle, in all markets, apart from the centrally-planned economies. The competitive situation has some features in common with a zero-sum game: an advance for one company can be regarded as a lost opportunity for the other companies. The participants follow each others' activities carefully and imitate behaviour which appears likely to lead to further successes.

Maintaining a position in foreign markets is no longer a disadvantage. The Swedish companies — and this applies to all the sectors studied — are the most internationalised of all the competitors. Assessments made by the Swedish companies and their competitors indicate that 'the Swedes' in many cases now have an advantage over their foreign competitors in the form of broader experience in establishing and operating subsidiaries in foreign countries. This is probably because the Swedish companies were forced to expand into foreign markets at a considerably earlier stage than their competitors, which normally had access to larger domestic markets.

The manufacturers' role has been to supply buyers with systems offering technologically advanced and reliable solutions to their production problems. The economics of the situation are obviously important to the buyers, but buyers are primarily concerned with 'total economics', viewed over rather long periods of time. Against this perspective, possible stand-still time costs become highly significant. In this sort of situation, the price of the system supplied is only one factor amongst many influencing the financial outcome for the purchasers. In addition, in cases where the system presented by competitors differs in many respects from the Swedish offering and where it does become difficult to make direct price comparisons, price is unlikely to be the central competitive argument. Research and development and marketing — marketing in a very broad sense — tend to dominate the picture. As we have suggested previously, it is a question of creating relationships as close as possible with the buyers by means of product adaptation, problem-solving and training and service programmes.

Most of the foreign manufacturing investments made by Swedish companies have continued to have the objective of supplying the local market, even in the relatively late stages of the process which are considered here. However, it should also be noted that there are some typical patterns which are associated with these advanced phases in operations.

Surviving small competitors become attractive propositions for acquisitions. A small campany may, for example, have developed a speciality which proves useful. From the point of view of large companies which aim to maintain a broad product range in order to be able to offer solutions for as many needs as possible within the field chosen, a take-over may be a quicker way to achieve results than painfully acquiring competence from a low starting point. An appropriate example here is Atlas Copco's acquisition of the American company Jarva, which is one of an extremely limited number of companies which have developed what are known as 'gallery drilling techniques', so as to avoid drilling a large number of holes in the required area and using explosive charges.

Taking over a competitor with an established trade mark and established relationships with certain buyers is a relatively quick, and probably cheap, way of increasing market shares. Sandvik's purchase of Le Burin in France is one example of this type of market-share acquisition.

However, acquisition should not only be seen in terms of the aggressive advancement of comparitive positions — there is also a defensive aspect. It is not just a question of a short-term change in the competitive situation, as in Sandvik's case which involved possible price-cuts on the French market if the smaller company 'fell into the hands of' one of Sandvik's major competitors. Such a change also involves an advancement of competitive positions which might well have negative consequences in the long term on other markets.

We have previously described the establishment of manufacturing subsidiaries, the aim of which is to supply a local market, as a stage in the internationalisation process of the company. The post-war liberalisation of international trade, combined with the increased size of internationalised companies, has led us into the next phase in the internationalisation process. Newly-established or existing manufacturing subsidiaries now often specialise in the manufacture of certain items in the product range, destined for a wider market than the host country can offer.

Atlas Copco and Fläkt are examples of organisations which have already moved into this internationalisation phase. Thus Atlas Copco's Bremen plant is the group supplier of drillings. Similarly, Fläkt's French subsidiary manufactures fans while the Belgian subsidiary is responsible for heat exchangers used by the West German subsidiary for the assembly of air-conditioning equipment which is then, in turn, supplied to most Western European markets.

It is not a question, at this stage, of utilising company-specific advantages in the struggle with local competitors for a local market. Instead, it is a question of minimising costs in order to supply sales organisations with the products they require. The country-specific characteristics are therefore important in this context and it is primarily the country-specific advantages — including geographical distance to the point of sale — which determine localisation (at least in the case of new investments). Atlas Copco's location of production in Bremen was considerably influenced by the availability of skilled and well-trained labour. Since companies with international operations have knowledge and experience of conditions in a wide range of countries, they can choose 'rationally' between various locations on the basis of the characteristics of the production process involved. It may also be advantageous to split up a production process if the manufacturing phases have different characteristics, in accordance with the country-specific advantages of various countries.

However, a much more typical way of redistributing production activities is where companies cease to manufacture certain relatively simple components and instead purchase them from independent, specialised manufacturers. Swedish manufacturers do not always have sufficiently large volumes to justify continued manufacturing of all components themselves.

In certain cases, internal specialisation within the group may mean that a foreign subsidiary becomes more important than the corresponding Swedish unit, in the case of a specific product. Group management may then consider it advantageous also to transfer management responsibility and research and development activities for the product to the foreign subsidiary. This has not happened to any appreciable extent in the industrial sectors we have studied, but in other sectors there are several examples. In the case of Sandvik's steel conveyor division, management administration and the major part of research and development activities have been moved to the West German subsidiary. Divisional management and research and development in the Atlas Copco compressor division are centred on the group's Belgian subsidiary, which is the dominant manufacturing unit for this group of products. This type of change may be regarded as a further phase in the internationalisation process.

The fact that some company groups — or rather divisions within such groups — have pursued the internationalisation process described above, involving location of managerial responsibility for some operations in a foreign subsidiary, does not mean that all companies are likely to follow the same path. Some companies will continue to find it most advantageous to supply foreign markets by exporting from Sweden. Other companies will continue to have subsidiaries which only supply their local market.

It is interesting to note that development, in a few cases, has meant moving into a new industry. Sandvik, which started as a steel company, now has its major area of operations in cemented carbide, involving, for example, the manufacture of cutting-tools for the engineering industry. As a result of vertical integration in the contracting and installation field, the centre of gravity in Fläkt's case has come to lie in these areas and Fläkt, in point of fact, could not today be termed an industrial company in simple, one-dimensional terms. Although there are several reasons for these developments, of course, it is clear that the increased marketing emphasis in these companies has played an important role in both cases.

In common with many other observers of industrial development, we feel that we have been able to trace increased cooperation between companies — not only at the vertical level, but also horizontally. We find, for example, Ericsson's cooperation with a competitor in the expansion of the telephone network in a large market, developing a new product in collaboration with another competitor and selling parts of the product range of a third competitor in certain markets, etc. Thus, the reason for such cooperation varies from case to case. However, one common factor seems to be a desire to limit costs, especially for research and development. In addition, cooperation no doubt contributes to improving stability and predictability in the area of competition.

The question is now what the fourth phase may involve. Naturally, it is tempting to extrapolate and predict continued concentration — a concentration not necessarily achieved as the result of a reduction in the number of surviving companies. Similar effects may be achieved through increased cooperation.

However, it is also possible that the pattern of development we have seen in the telecommunications equipment industry will become increasingly typical. New technology, electronics in this case, has led to the development of a telephone exchange which is a computer adapted for telephony. The applications can be changed with relative ease so that not only communications, but also data processing, etc., can be accomplished within the framework of the system. Frontiers between a number of industries have disappeared, or are in the process of disappearing. Naturally the market for companies operating in this type of new industry will expand enormously, but the number of competitors will also increase. A completely new situation is occurring and therefore it may not be at all relevant to speak of a fourth phase in the development process of the telephone equipment industry — we should, perhaps, speak of the birth of a new industry.

Comments

What is, in fact the value of this model, assuming that it has a certain validity? The first point is that it may contribute to a clarification of certain links between changes at industry, sector and company levels — such as internationalisation, for example. Secondly, the model has proved to be useful from the pedagogic angle when, for example, trying to explain internationalisation as an integrated aspect of industrial development. This approach then becomes a central factor in demonstrating the dynamic effects of direct investments. Finally, the model has proved to be useful in discussions with top management about current and future developments in their industries and in their companies. Further research is required, of course, to refine the model and determine the limits of its validity.

Notes

1. We may mention that in other sectors where Fläkt is active, global competition does exist — for example, in the field of equipment used in industrial research.
2. Since direct investments have normally been associated with general growth, actual physical transfer of operations has not actually been involved. Instead, it has been a case of expansion of capacity being located in a foreign market rather than in Sweden.

6 MODELS FOR EVALUATING THE IMPACT OF FOREIGN DIRECT INVESTMENT

An essential condition for any analysis of effects is that the causal relationships in the area studied are known. These relationships are very complicated where the effects of foreign direct investments are concerned. Foreign direct investments are, in fact, not an exogenous factor in the economy, that is to say not the ultimate reasons for various effects. Various conditions in the companies' environment, instead, can explain, or can be regarded as the reasons for, decisions which the company takes on foreign investments (see Figure 6.1). The factors which give rise to direct investments may also be regarded as reasons for other phenomena, not related to direct investments, for example concentration, specialisation and foreign trade. Direct investments are thus one of the several 'primary' effects which are the result of more basic causes, such as foreign trade policy, technical development and other factors which regulate conditions for doing business. The other primary effects can then, in turn, be regarded as reasons for the 'secondary' effects which we attempt to measure.

To summarise, causal relationships are unclear, partly because direct investments are not the intrinsic cause of economic effects, and partly because these effects also result from other factors partly related to direct investments. This is why empirical studies, in the past, have normally looked at only a few out of the many possible effects. Furthermore, these empirical studies have employed varying methods which have differed not only as regards their theoretical basis, but also in terms of whether the analysis was short-term or long-term, whether a specific investment was studied or several, and whether the effects were studied from the point of view of the company undertaking the investment or from the point of view of the total economy. In this chapter, we will first discuss methods which have been used previously to determine the effects of direct investments. We will then describe the methodological considerations applied in this study.

60

Figure 6.1: Foreign Direct Investment as an Integrated Part of the Economic System

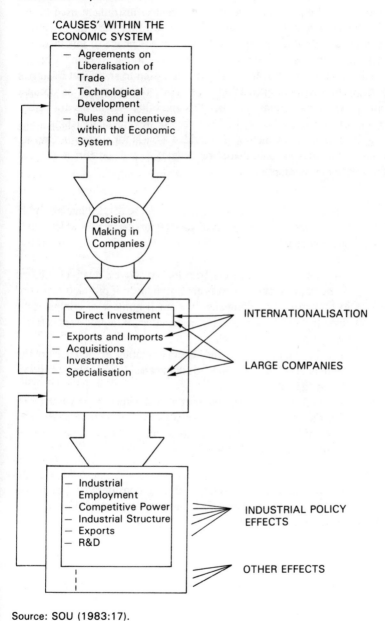

Source: SOU (1983:17).

Direct Investment in Neo-Classical Equilibrium Theory

Neo-classical equilibrium theory is the central instrument used to explain behaviour in the economic system and to measure the effects of such behaviour at the macro level. A great advantage of this theory is that the analysis describes the whole economic system. General equilibrium theory has, for example, been used to show that countries gain by trading with each other. Free trade thus becomes an optimal policy. The assumptions on which this and other statements are based, if the theory is to be applicable, are, however, far-reaching. The equilibrium models which have provided a basis for studies in international economics include, therefore, several — and sometimes all — of the following assumptions:

(a)   The production of goods and demand can be divided into a number of homogeneous groupings of goods (markets) within which goods are completely interchangeable. A corresponding division can also be made between factors of production.

(b)   No economies of scale can be achieved above a relatively limited scale of production — costs are not reduced if production is concentrated on one company or a small number of companies.

(c)   Information about products and manufacturing processes is freely accessible and available.

(d)   There are many buyers and sellers operating in each market and there are no tendencies towards dominance (monopoly or oligopoly) in the market.

(e)   All markets operate without friction and without transaction costs. It is therefore possible for the analysis to concentrate on description of (and comparison between) various conditions of equilibrium in the economy.

These assumptions are at variance — often at considerable variance — with conditions in the real world. Considerable research effort in the neo-classical research tradition has therefore been devoted to testing the effects of modifications of these assumptions and determining how national economic policies should be designed if these modifications are taken into account (Corden, 1974b).

In an article which received wide attention, Macdoughall (1960) undertook a theoretical analysis of the effects of direct investments, employing neo-classical theory. Macdoughall started out from the assumption that direct investments mean that the volume of capital stocks in the countries concerned is influenced. The analysis concludes that the host country profits from such investments, since tax revenues are higher, and that positive external effects are achieved chiefly through the dissemination of know-how and the pressure on domestic companies to increase their productivity. The country making the investment also profits, since the home country achieves a higher yield on capital than would have been the case otherwise. The failure to invest in the home country's economy leads to lower productivity of labour than would otherwise have been the case, but the home country, none the less, achieves a total net economic gain. Thus, both countries profit from such direct investment. Macdoughall's analysis is based on a number of assumptions, such as full employment, no transaction costs, no economies of scale and free competition in the sense that no seller is sufficiently powerful to influence the functioning of the market. One by one, Macdoughall abandons these assumptions, considering that his conclusions do not need to be fundamentally changed as a result of his modified assumptions. However, a test of the effects of a simultaneous removal of all the assumptions is not undertaken and, as far as is known, no such test has been applied by any other economist.

A great deal of the voluminous research carried out in the field of multinational corporations in the 1960s and 1970s was based on a neo-classical frame of reference. A well-known example is Musgrave's (1975) study for a congressional committee on the effects of the outflow of American direct investments. It would therefore be justified to take the view that official attitudes and policies as regards multinational companies and foreign direct investments are largely based on results arrived at within the neo-classical tradition.

Contra-Factual Analysis

The central question in many of the studies which have looked at the effects of direct investments is how events which have actually been observed deviate from what otherwise might have occurred (Bergsten *et al.*, 1978, p. 6). We would define contra-factual analyses as various studies which attempt, in some explicit way, to form an opinion as to what would have happened if the company had been forced to choose the second best alternative. This method of analysis has been used primarily to determine export and employment effects. What has then been done is to attempt to evaluate what alternatives to direct investment companies have had, if it is assumed that a certain product is to be sold on a certain foreign market. Normally the alternative would have been exports from the domestic market or, as a less preferable alternative, some form of licensing agreement. The results arrived at as regards export opportunities depend on an assessment of how foreign production influences the company's sales on the foreign market *and* to what extent foreign manufacturing depends on raw materials and semi-finished goods, and on finished products originating in the home country.

This type of analysis is normally based on neo-classical equilibrium theory and makes the further assumption that the home country has more or less fixed exchange rates and a free exchange of goods and capital with the outside world. Increased exports then become a sign that the country's international competitive strength is on the increase which means that the country regains its former postion if there has been a deficit in the balance of exchange, or is able to take further political measures requiring economic resources, if the country was already in balance on its foreign trade. Increased employment implies better utilisation of resources, assuming some initial unemployment. When employment figures change, there may also be shifts between different types of labour involved, depending on the nature of the foreign investments. Thus, in brief, an 'effect' in the form of increased exports means that the country's international competitive position has improved. Such increased exports take place mainly as a result of better utilisation of existing and available production resources, which leads to higher industrial employment. If export and employment changes do not move in the same direction, this may be the result of price changes or rationalisation.

The first, and perhaps best known, measurements of effects based on contra-factual analysis were carried out in Britain by Reddaway *et al.*, (1968), and in the United States by Hufbauer and Adler (1968). The common factor in these studies was that they examined the balance of payments and export effects of direct investment outflows. The British study did not undertake a particularly sophisticated analysis of what would have happened in the alternative situation. It was assumed, quite simply, that if the investment had not taken place abroad it would not have taken place domestically either. Hufbauer and Adler used a somewhat more advanced analysis, considering three different alternatives:

(i)   Investment means an addition to the host country's volume of investment and a corresponding reduction in the home country. One example might be where a company has a unique product and must decide whether to make the production investment either in the home country or abroad (the classical case).

(ii) In this case it is assumed that investment would have occurred in the host country anyway, but would than have been undertaken by another company, domestic or foreign. The investment volume in the home country is not affected. An example might be a company which invests abroad to reinforce a position in the market or to get inside a high tariff wall. Such investments are usually termed, in fact, 'market oriented' or 'defensive' (the reversed classical case).

(iii) In any other situation, the investment would not have taken place, either in the host country or in the home country. Here we have a combination of a certain specific company and a specific country which makes the investment profitable (the anti-classical case).

In the first case, it could be said that the multinational company is in a superior position in relation to other companies. In the second case, it is the host country or the foreign market which has all the best cards. It may be that the host country demands local production of any company which wishes to sell there or, perhaps, that the host country offers obvious advantages when compared with other countries, such as lower wages, cheaper raw materials or, quite simply, greater demand. Thus, in the British study, it was assumed that all foreign investments were of this type. In practice, it is seldom possible to distinguish the alternatives so clearly — the normal situation is probably, in fact, that the background to an investment is a combination of company and market factors.

Both studies were criticised, for example by Dunning (1969). Dunning considered that the assumptions lying behind the discussion of alternatives were oversimplified and ignored important aspects, such as an improvement of the competitive position of a company undertaking investments in a foreign market. In addition, Dunning considered that the data used in the studies were inadequate, which meant that the results arrived at were somewhat difficult to assess.

The Hufbauer and Adler study was followed by several others which used similar approaches in attempting to measure the effects of direct investments on employment in the United States. In several of the American studies the total effects on employment can be placed under three headings:

(i) Production effects — the reduction in employment resulting from the sale of goods which are manufactured abroad rather than in the home country. This effect is greater the more it is assumed that it would have been possible to export these goods if production had not been established abroad. On the other hand, if the market had been closed without such establishment, there would, of course, be no loss of production and no reduction in employment. In the first case the production effect will always be negative, and in the second case the production effect will be zero.

(ii) Export stimulation effects — subsidiaries purchase equipment and components from the home country in varying degrees, which influences the volume of production and employment in the home country. This effect is always positive.

(iii) Administration effects — the parent company's establishment abroad places demands on the additional services of various administrators, consultants and specialists in the company and also in other companies. This effect is also always positive.

Another attempt to develop the techniques of contra-factual analysis is made by Frank and Freeman (1978) in their examination of export effects. Their objective was to explain to what extent exports from United States would have taken place if American subsidiaries had not undertaken manufacturing overseas. Frank and Freeman were obliged to make two important assumptions in answering this question. The first assumption involved the question of how much more expensive goods would have been on foreign markets if manufacturing had taken place on the home market and the goods had then been exported. The second assumption involved the extent of a decline in demand in the foreign market when the price for a good rises. Both these assumptions are difficult to cope with, especially the latter. Frank and Freeman's analysis has been criticised because it attempts to estimate the price sensitivity of the market using internal company cost data and because it does not take into account the situation where a foreign investment can be seen as an offensive measure which can give rise to exports which otherwise would not have taken place (Bergsten *et al.*, 1978, p. 98).

The problem with the research discussed above is that it is difficult to estimate the long-term effects, since an economy without foreign investment and without multinational companies would have been rather different. This comment is, of course, especially relevant for a small country such as Sweden, with a high level of dependence on foreign countries. However, Niehans (1977) has employed a quite different approach in an analysis of the Swiss economy. The analysis was carried out in three stages where the first stage specified the conditions which

limit direct investments. Niehans assumed, on the one hand, that all artificial barriers to trade, which are the most important reason for direct
investments, would be eliminated and, on the other hand, that all countries would stop international investments by employing various legal
means. The second stage in Niehans's analysis was to study how such
changed conditions would affect a number of Swiss multinational companies and the third stage was to look at how this would then affect the
Swiss economy.

The result of the analysis of the effects of reduced protectionism
resulting from the elimination of trade barriers was that multinational
corporations would still exist, but there would be fewer of them and that
they would be smaller. Without protectionism, the Swiss companies
would be smaller but would still achieve satisfactory financial results.
The Swiss economy would also gain from a non-protectionist situation.

The effects of a prohibition on direct investments, while still permit-
ting international trade, would be extremely negative. The companies
studied would be reduced to small enterprises or would disappear completely. In support of this view, it was pointed out that there is no major
export company in existence which does not manufacture abroad. The
main effect, according to Niehans, would be a loss of scale advantages.
If multinational companies did not exist, there would be a high correlation between the size of the home market and the size of the companies.
Large countries would still be able to boast large companies, while small
countries would only have small or medium-sized corporations. Niehans
concluded that international investments contribute to a levelling out of
the differences between small and large countries. He does not, therefore,
regard direct investment as a weapon used by large countries to achieve
economic dominance, but rather as a way for smaller countries to assert
themselves.

Hufbauer & Adler's and Niehans's analyses of effects can be considered as extreme cases, as regards the assumptions made about the
alternatives if there is no direct investment. Hufbauer and Adler's analysis
assumes that everything else is unchanged if the foreign investment does
not take place. Niehans, on the other hand, attempts to estimate the effects which would result if the whole world changed its attitude towards
world trade and direct investments. Thus it is clear that both types of
analyses are based on unrealistic assumptions. A direct investment will
not 'disappear' unless something else happens in the economy, but, on
the other hand, the effects of direct investments on a small country such
as Sweden must, of course, be based on the assumption that what happens to Swedish investments has very little influence on the outside world.

The most realistic assumption for the analysis of effects might be to base the discussion on minor or limited regulations of direct investments undertaken unilaterally by Sweden. Other situations would seem to be of purely theoretical interest.

Company Comparisons

An alternative method of forming an opinion on the effects of direct investments is to compare multinational companies operations with those of national companies. The advantage of such comparisons over contrafactual analyses is that it is not necessary to use hypothetical information since comparison can be based on two sets of factual data. The problem is simply that it is difficult to find comparable populations as an object of study and that possible differences cannot be directly translated into 'effects'. As regards the primary question of which companies should be compared, it is, of course, hazardous to assume that there would only have been companies which resemble today's national companies if there had been no direct investments. In other words, are there systematic differences between companies which invest abroad and others that do not, which are not due to foreign activities? One method of approaching a solution to this methodological problem is to break down the data so that the companies compared are as similar as possible in all other ways except those relating to their foreign operations. The problem is that this does not take us very far, since the multinationals quite simply do not have national equivalents. This is illustrated in the following example.

In 1979, an ILO report was presented describing the effects that foreign-owned companies had had on employment in Belgium (Van den Bulcke and Halsberghe, 1979). The report attempted to show the increase in industrial employment which resulted from the establishment by foreign companies of manufacturing operations in Belgium and was based on data gathered in the course of two studies of all foreign-owned companies in Belgium in 1968 and 1975.

Investments by the foreign companies were estimated to have led to an additional 80,000–130,000 jobs. The figures on additional employment cannot however be interpreted to mean that employment would have been at least 80,000 jobs less if foreign companies had *not* invested or had not been active in Belgium. It is not possible to know what would have otherwise happened in the investment field. In an attempt to evaluate the increasing employment which took place in the foreign companies, this increase was compared with the corresponding change in employment, both for all industrial companies in Belgium and for the group of Belgian companies which did not include the multinational Belgian concerns.

In the 1971-6 period (not the same period as previously), employment in the foreign-owned companies increased by 9 per cent while, in the Belgian companies, employment fell by 4 per cent. However, employment in the group of Belgian companies without foreign subsidiaries increased by 1 per cent. As a result, the total decline in employment was explained as a consequence of a reduced number of employees in the Belgian multinational corporations.

Since the study included a wide range of data about the companies, it was possible to study whether other factors varied in sympathy with the increase in employment. The most important result which emerged was that employment had developed in very different ways in different industries and that the foreign-owned companies did not have the same degree of participation in different industries as the Belgian companies. If it could be assumed hypothetically that the foreign companies had had the same industrial dispersion as all Belgian companies, employment would have only increased by 1 per cent instead of 9 per cent. Only one of the other company characteristics studied varied in sympathy with the increase in employment for all three categories of companies: yield on capital. The foreign-owned companies also had a higher proportion of extremely profitable companies than the other two categories. The Belgian study can be regarded as an example of the so-called comparative method. Generally speaking, the result of such studies, as in this case, is that the foreign-owned companies achieve a greater increase in employment than domestic companies. However, it could also be concluded that the increase in employment in Belgian industry took place mainly in certain industries and in companies with high profitability. The foreign-owned companies were more extensively represented in the expansive industries and had higher profitability than the Belgian companies and therefore also achieved a greater increase in employment. The result of the Belgian study could also be said to indicate that multinational and national companies are different and that perhaps it is not plausible to attempt to neutralise the effects of, for example, varying degrees of participation in certain industries. A comparison between multinational and national companies only demonstrates the characteristics of each category but gives us no certain indication of what would happen if one category was replaced by the other.

Even if we disregard the problem of comparability between the categories, we are still left with the problem of determining and interpreting possible differences. The determination of what are the significant differences between various companies' profitability, expansion, etc., is largely a question of statistics. But even if the problem can be solved by using statistical techniques the question of interpretation of the differences in company performance remains — and here we are faced by two different possible views. Perhaps the most common view is that profitable and expanding companies are 'better' than less profitable companies. Therefore, when it is observed that multinational companies achieve higher profits, this is regarded as proof that they represent a positive factor in the global economy. On the other hand, if we take theory of industrial organisation as our starting point, high profitability may in fact be regarded as an expression of a monopolistic situation and thus constitutes a negative effect. It is not possible to state, in general terms, which interpretation is correct — the question of whether high profitability should be regarded as positive or negative must be decided from case to case with due consideration to the structure of the industry in the specific instance studied.

To summarise, we can observe that statistical studies of large populations of companies, both with, and without, direct foreign investments, are necessary in any survey of the importance and extent of the operations of international corporations. The differences between categories of companies as regards the intensity of research and development, growth, employment, etc., are also undoubtedly what we called secondary effects earlier in this chapter. The problem is that it is not possible to trace such effects simply back to direct investments. The statistical differences between categories of companies can thus not be used indiscriminately to arrive at conclusions about what would have happened if direct investments had not taken place. What we can say, rather, is what the industrial structure looks like with an economic system which contains, for example, multinational companies.

Econometric Methods

A third technique which can be used in studying the effects of foreign direct investments is analysis using econometric methods. One advantage of econometrics is that it permits the processing of a greater volume of data than other techniques. Econometric methods are used, for example, to attempt to answer the question of how much exports increase or fall as a result of companies' increasing their production abroad. The result of an analysis of this type, which examines the correlation between two variables cannot, however, be used indiscriminately to draw conclusions about what actually would happen if direct investments increased or decreased. One reason is that the volume of exports is influenced by other factors — not just the volume of foreign direct investment. In addition, there is a mutual correlation between exports and direct investments which means that a high level of exports can increase the likelihood that direct investment would take place.

In regression analysis, it must also be assumed that all correlations between direct investment and exports are of the same type. The export effect is, however, probably different if we compare the case of a former sales company which starts to manufacture on its own account and a case where direct investment takes the form of the acquisition of an existing foreign company. There may also be systematic differences between direct investments which take place at an early stage or at a late stage in the internationalisation process of a corporation. In the early stages of the internationalisation process, the parent company is still completely dominant. As activities are progressively shifted abroad, organisational changes in the corporation follow. A new subsidiary in a corporation which has already proceeded a long way on the path to internationalisation can therefore be expected to produce effects which differ, both for the host country and for the home country, from those which resulted from the establishment of the first foreign subsidiary. Econometric methods, however, are only concerned with a historical, average correlation between foreign production and exports. The critical methodological question is whether this correlation changes to such an extent over time that the measurement of effects becomes unreliable and uncertain.

Methodological Considerations in DIRK's Studies

The methods for determining the effects of foreign direct investments hitherto presented all have both advantages and disadvantages. As a result, when the Swedish government's Committee on Foreign Direct Investment (DIRK) commenced its work it was decided to use several methods in parallel. The conclusions presented in the following chapter can therefore be said to represent a collective assessment of the results of several methods and approaches. In common with many others who have tried to determine the effects of direct investments, we have defined 'effect' as the difference between what has actually happened after direct investment has taken place, for example in terms of the volume of sales in a certain country, and what would have happened if the company had done something else, probably exporting directly from the home country. We do not want to limit ourselves, however, to making stereotyped assumptions about alternative situations since our ambition has been to discuss the alternatives in greater depth and with greater realism. The fact that previous studies have yielded such varying results is largely due to the different assumptions which have been made as regards the alternatives to foreign investments.

Of the five studies undertaken, two have involved a small number of companies or groups of companies where two or three direct investments have been studied in detail, set against the background of the companies' development on the broader horizon. Some twenty companies have been used as cases in the studies — mostly Swedish multinational companies. The selection of objects for study has not been made on a random basis. An attempt was made to include many of the major foreign investors — mostly in the engineering industry. However, a few examples of investments which are less typical from the Swedish point of view have also been studied — for example the manufacture of clothing in countries with low wage levels. The study, which is focused on industrial sectors, utilises a frame of reference which includes elements of industrial organisation and direct investment theory (SOU, 1981:33). The other study, where the emphasis is on individual companies, is largely based on the concept of advantages which are specific to each country as an explanatory factor for direct investments, but also includes an examination of micro-theoretical models for measurement of effects (SOU, 1981:43).

Three broader descriptive studies were undertaken, in parallel with the two reports, which are designed to formulate hypotheses. One of the descriptive studies covers the development of multinational, foreign-owned and national companies in Sweden (SOU, 1982:15). The second examines Swedish multinational companies and their foreign operations (SOU, 1982:27), while the third describes changes in employment in Swedish industry in terms of functions and levels of skill and competence (SOU, 1983:16). The three studies are not based on samples but cover what are virtually total populations. Apart from the intrinsic value of the descriptions, they are also used in combination with the results of case and industrial sector studies to develop conclusions about the direction of the more aggregated effects of direct investments.

A special problem, which is closely linked with the question of the alternative situation for direct investments, is that it is legally possible to achieve virtually the same object without having recourse to direct investments. Thus, a Swedish company may enter into an agreement with a foreign company stating that the latter foreign organisation will fulfil the same functions as a subsidiary would have done. As will be described later, Swedish companies in the clothing industry not only have their own production units abroad but also employ foreign suppliers who comply with the same type of instructions as received by subsidiaries. In many cases production agreements are not a full alternative to direct investment but none the less come so close that we have not made any distinction in the analysis of effects between a direct investment and a possible alternative production agreement.

Depending on the purpose of a specific direct investment, an alternative has thus been formulated, implying that production would if possible have been undertaken in Sweden instead and the products then exported. This approach has been criticised, however, because it is said that the results of a contra-factual analysis of this type can only be positive. The critics maintain that the analysis should instead be undertaken so that direct investment is compared with efforts devoted to other business concepts or methods, such as investments in the research and development function or in the acquisition of market shares on the domestic market. This might well be theoretically possible, but it would require that new business propositions were developed in the study, followed by a financial analysis of the consequences. It is unlikely that such superior alternatives would be found. In any event, the analysis would require very extensive assumptions. From the point of view of the principle involved, it is worth noting that companies do not themselves develop such alternatives. In the investment decision, various types of investment alternatives are seldom compared against each other. Attention tends to be paid to the alternatives successively and the question raised is whether they are sufficiently advantageous or not — not whether they are better than other theoretically possible investments.

Another objection to our contra-factual analysis is that it does not include unsuccessful direct investments. There are examples of failures, but judging by the number of discontinued subsidiaries abroad and what is revealed by the corporate financial reports, the number of unsuccessful attempts at establishment is relatively few. As regards the important question of whether the results of these studies can be used to form an opinion about possible changes in policies for direct investment, it is of course very much a question of whether one believes that history repeats itself. Many observers believe, however, that the remarkable period of economic development after the Second World War has been largely a one-off effect of the liberalisation of world trade and of international investments. The unmistakeable signs of increased protectionism may lead to considerable changes, above all for world trade, but also, indirectly, for international investments. It is hard to predict what the effects of these changes will be for the countries concerned in a more tightly regulated world economy, but it is not at all unlikely that the effects will be different from those we have experienced hitherto.

Notes

1. Mundell (1975) has shown that factor movements can be perfect substitutes for trade in goods and that foreign direct investments, under certain conditions have the same effects as international trade.

PART TWO:

IMPACT OF FOREIGN DIRECT INVESTMENT ON
SWEDISH INDUSTRY

7 TECHNOLOGICAL DEVELOPMENT

Discussion of the effects of foreign direct investments amounts to a description of various changes in Swedish industry resulting from direct investments. These changes are not, of course, mutually independent. Technological development can result in better products and more efficient production processes which improve the competitive position of companies, providing opportunities for exports and continued technological development, etc. Even if such effects can be viewed as different aspects of the same phenomenon, we find ourselves obliged to present them separately. The effects of foreign direct investments which we have studied concern technological development, international competitiveness, exports, employment and the structure of the industry. Part Two concludes with an attempt to arrive at a total assessment.

Most technological development takes place within the company sector. If we employ the data of the Swedish Central Bureau of Statistics for technological and scientific research in Sweden in 1977 as a measure, we find that industry was responsible for 60 per cent of research. The remaining research activities were conducted by universities and other publicly financed institutions. The emphasis on practical applications in the objectives of publicly and privately financed research varies considerably. To illustrate this, it is customary to split up research and development activities (R&D) into three areas:

 (i)   basic research (i.e. research which is carried out without any im-
       mediate practical applications in view);
 (ii) applied research (i.e. research aiming at practical utilisation);
 (iii) development (i.e. the utilisation of research results to improve
       or create new products or techniques).

Publicly financed research is largely directed towards basic research, while privately financed operations have a greater emphasis on applied research and development. It has been estimated that, in American industry, basic research amounted to 15 per cent of total R&D expenditure, while 20 per cent was devoted to applied research, and 65 per cent to development (US Tariff Commission, 1973, p. 552).

In the industrial context, there has been some discussion of the

77

appropriate proportion of total resources inside the country on the various R&D areas. Should each country conduct basic research in proportion to its applied research, or is it possible to exploit basic research which takes place abroad? On the other hand, is it possible to stimulate industrial development in a country by expanding basic research? It has been said that American companies have been successful as regards the exploitation of research results originating both in the United States and in Europe. Although Europe has been in the lead in achieving important breakthroughs in basic research, practical applications have mainly taken place in American industry.

In contrast with the situation in basic research, the results of applied research and development are generally not widely disseminated or available. In order to stimulate companies to pursue technological development, practically all countries have accepted that inventors who contribute to technological know-how should have sole rights to the resultant financial advantages for a certain period of time. These monopoly rights can be guaranteed by means of patents and trade-mark protection, for example. Thus society accepts that expenditure on the extension of technological knowledge should imply an opportunity to finance development by means of sales revenues which are higher than the revenues which would have applied under free competition. A company's sole right to R&D results can, however, also involve the risk that knowledge is not effectively spread and utilised industrially in the most desirable way from the point of view of society at large. This problem is accentuated when a considerable proportion of technological development is carried out in companies which are active on an international front.

The effects of direct investments on Swedish technological developments are interesting from several points of view — for example, to what extent the existence of multinationals influences the extent and direction of development. Several studies conducted in other countries have confirmed that there is a correlation between foreign investments and the volume of R&D, and this is in full agreement with the theory covering the emergence of multinational corporations.

Another aspect that will be discussed is whether increased manufacturing activities by Swedish companies abroad lead to the switching of an increasing proportion of R&D activities outside Sweden. As regards foreign-owned companies in Sweden, the question is whether they undertake a reasonable proportion of their development work in Sweden — in line with the type and volume of total activities, etc. In the case of Swedish companies which have been taken over by foreign firms, it is instead interesting to study whether previous R&D activities have been affected by the change in ownership.

From the Swedish point of view, a shift of R&D operations to the foreign subsidiaries of multinational companies can be regarded as negative for a number of reasons. From a short-term perspective, the home country misses some of the positive spin-off effects which industrial R&D is said to have on other enterprises. Thus, industrial growth in Sweden would probably have been less than it actually has been if all R&D activities in the foreign multinational concerns had taken place in their home countries. We choose to ignore the fact that certain R&D operations abroad may have positive effects on the competitive status of the companies concerned.

Where international specialisation and concentration result in foreign subsidiaries' being given central responsibility for the development of a specific product, know-how about the product will decline, in a broad sense, in the home country. Furthermore, if specialisation also means that a company concentrates on some areas of the product range or simply on components used in final products, it is not possible to form an opinion about the country's degree of self-sufficiency by studying where the final product is manufactured or assembled. To date, this problem has mainly been discussed in the agricultural field where there are specific self-sufficiency goals for final products but where production is totally dependent on various types of imports.

Thus there are several reasons for maintaining that it is in the interest of Swedish industry that the R&D activities of Swedish multinational should be carried out in Sweden. This view may need to be modified where close contacts with foreign customers or foreign research-workers are important for R&D results. The same applies if local R&D operations are essential if the company is to sell on foreign markets. Before we discuss information about the localisation of R&D activities, we would like to mention briefly some of the reasons given by multinational companies for placing their R&D activities abroad. As an example, Sandvik justified its location of some R&D activities in the field of cemented carbide to Japan, Great Britain and the United States on the grounds that the company wished to undertake development in close proximity to its major industrial customers. A further reason for the transfer or the initiation of R&D operations at foreign production plants was that the host country authorities require such localisation. The location of Ericsson's R&D operations in Brazil and Italy have exactly this background. A third reason for the location of R&D activities abroad has been that expansion takes companies into areas where research in Sweden can be

regarded as a handicap. When Atlas Copco decided to begin selling products for drilling in soft geological formations, which are not found in
Sweden, the company chose to locate development of the new products
in Switzerland.

A third aspect of the correlation between direct investments and
technological development that will be discussed is how, and on what
terms, the multinational companies spread their technological know-how.
If research and development is to have effects at the industrial level,
it must of course lead to results that can be put into practice, for example new products, manufacturing processes or materials which ultimately
reach the market place. Multinational companies are not only regarded
as the heaviest investors in R&D, but they are also considered to be
especially well placed as disseminators of new technological knowledge.
Since multinationals already have international manufacturing and sales
organisations, they can rapidly spread their new technology — probably
at relatively low cost.

Even though multinational companies may be efficient instruments
for the distribution and spreading of technology, there are, none the less,
certain problems. One such problem is that developing countries may
find it difficult to absorb new technology in the form that it is marketed
by multinational corporations. The dissemination of technology by multinationals works best between societies or countries with similar conditions and needs. However, even as regards the spread of technology between developed countries, it has been noted in Canada that national R&D
needs to be of a certain size if it is to be possible to utilise foreign
technology (Information Canada, 1972). A special problem posed by the
import of technology is that in certain cases such technology may not
be utilised for product development and re-export. A case which achieved
wide publicity involved Datasaab's sale of flight control equipment to
Moscow in contravention of an export ban which applied to American
manufactured items used in the system.

There are a number of other aspects which might be of interest but
which we cannot analyse due to the absence of firmer information. The
Swedish Academy of Engineering Sciences (IVA) proposed, in a report
published a few years ago, that certain areas would be especially appropriate for investment by Swedish industry. This assessment was based
partly on Sweden's resources and relative advantages as regards industrial
and scientific competence and partly on important problem areas facing
Sweden, such as a considerable degree of dependence on imported energy
supplies. The interesting question is whether the fact that certain companies are involved in international operations makes it more difficult

to build up technological development in areas that were especially interesting from the Swedish point of view. Do Swedish multinational companies pay more attention to conditions on the world market than to specifically Swedish conditions and problems? Turning the problem the other way round, one might ask if foreign companies might consider technological development in areas that are especially relevant for industrial activities in Sweden.

As with most previous studies of this type, we have been obliged to measure technological development in terms of the costs or resources invested rather than to attempt to quantify the results of such development. One consequence of the measurement of development in terms of research costs or man-years is that it is impossible to arrive at any qualitative evaluation of the R&D activities carried out by the various companies.

Even if we limit ourselves to the study of what is invested in technological development, it may be difficult to obtain correct and balanced information. The available statistics tend to concentrate on activities carried out in specific development functions in companies. Since it is the larger companies which tend to have special development departments, it is possible that the contributions made by major companies in development activities are overestimated in the data. Development work in smaller companies presumably takes place alongside routine manufacturing and sales operations. It may also be the case that the smaller companies more often use know-how or technology which is widely available or purchased from other companies.

Volume and Emphasis of R&D in Multinational Corporations

All the available information indicates that companies with production abroad have more extensive R&D operations than other corporations. If we look initially at the total R&D costs for Swedish industry of 4,600 million kronor in 1978, Swedish multinational companies were responsible for 70 per cent of the total,[1] foreign-owned companies for 5 per cent and other Swedish companies for 25 per cent. As a comparison, Swedish multinational companies accounted for 48 per cent of Swedish industrial employment in 1978.

As regards the proportion of companies, by category, undertaking R&D activities, the figures indicate that 88 per cent of the Swedish multinational companies and 27 per cent of other Swedish companies conducted such operations (SIND, 1980:4). Information about the average intensity of R&D in the various corporate categories can be interpreted as indicating that R&D was of greater importance for multinational companies. R&D intensity has been calculated as the relationship between R&D costs and the value added in the respective company groupings, and the following figures were obtained: Swedish multinational companies, 6.4 per cent; foreign-owned companies, 3.3 per cent; Swedish national companies, 1.5 per cent. (SOU, 1982:15).

Since a considerable proportion of the Swedish national companies state that they do not conduct any R&D activities at all, we have also calculated the R&D intensity exclusively for companies in the various categories which have actually booked costs for technical development. The difference between the categories described previously remains unaffected, broadly speaking. This is indicated by Figure 7.1, showing how R&D intensity has changed in the period 1973–9.

Swedish multinationals and foreign-owned companies are roughly at the same level amongst companies conducting R&D activities. They have approximately three times as great an R&D intensity as the national companies. There are, however, considerable differences between companies in the foreign-owned category.[2] Acquired companies (i.e. companies previously Swedish-owned) reduced the average, while the corporations formed through greenfield investments increased their R&D costs more than any other group.

As a further safeguard to ensure that foreign production is related to the amount of technological development, we have attempted to neutralise the influence of two other factors which might influence R&D intensity: industry and size. Table 7.1 indicates that R&D intensity, expressed here as man-years of R&D in relation to the total number of employees, varies between different industries and size classes. The most interesting point is, however, that the previous difference between Swedish multinationals and other Swedish companies remains broadly unchanged even where comparison is made between companies of similar size in the same industry. The exception is primarily in the non-metalliferous mining industry (ISIC 36) where national companies demonstrate the highest levels of intensity. In the clothing industry (ISIC 32) the medium-sized multinational and national companies have approximately the same R&D intensity. When the number of companies compared is small, however, product differences in the industry may be the reason for variations in R&D. Thus the ISIC 32 industry includes both clothing companies and also companies manufacturing hygiene products made of textile materials.

Figure 7.1: Intensity of Companies' R&D Activities, 1973-7 and 1977-9

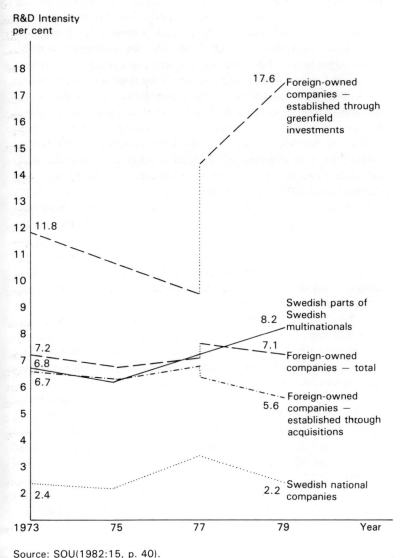

Source: SOU(1982:15, p. 40).
Note: Due to changes in population, figures from before and after 1977 are not comparable. R&D intensity is measured as R&D costs as a percentage of value added. The population includes only companies which have actually booked costs for R&D.

When we come to the question of whether multinational companies emphasise long-term R&D to a greater, or lesser, extent than other companies, our information indicates that there do not seem to be any noticeable differences between various categories of companies. Thus the Swedish national companies have a similar proportion of long-term R&D to the multinationals (SOU, 1982:15). An interpretation of this result might be that R&D inevitably consists of certain long-term activities and also of somewhat more significant short-term development work. What distinguishes the various company categories is not the proportions of various types of R&D activities, but rather the total extent of intensity of R&D operations.

It is reasonable to assume that direct investments influence foreign sales which, in turn, permit technological development, since high R&D activities presumes international sales. Indeed one of the studies found that the most R&D intensive companies have a strong tendency to supply foreign markets with exports from Sweden and not via foreign production (SOU, 1982:27, p. 171).[3] A possible explanation of this phenomenon is provided by product-cycle theory which states that R&D activities are largely integrated with the manufacturing process in the early stages of product or process development. Since R&D costs then constitute a major proportion of the price of the product, the difference in manufacturing costs between various countries is not very important. Therefore manufacturing is associated with R&D activities which are located in the home country. As the product becomes more standardised, price is increasingly significant which means that trade barriers, and possibly higher manufacturing costs in Sweden, make local manufacture relatively more advantageous.

Another possible interpretation of the negative relationship between R&D intensity and the proportion of production abroad, mentioned above, might be that R&D intensity drops as the company expands, and in such cases this expansion is likely to take place abroad. Alternative explanations, which do not rely on the product-cycle theory, can also be suggested. Thus it may be that the most research-intensive companies are to be found in limited product markets, where foreign production is rarely a viable alternative. This applies to the small pharmaceutical companies for example, which often only have a few internationally marketable products with sales volumes which do not justify local manufacture, although local manufacture would have been advantageous or is even required (as in France).

Table 7.1: R&D Intensity (R&D measured in man-years/total no. of employees) in All Companies in the Same Category in 1973 and 1977

Category	No. of Employees	ISIC 31		ISIC 32		ISIC 33		ISIC 34		ISIC 35		ISIC 36		ISIC 37		ISIC 38		ISIC 3	
		1973	1977	1973	1977	1973	1977	1973	1977	1973	1977	1973	1977	1973	1977	1973	1977	1973	1977
Swedish multi-nationals	< 200	—	—	0.0	0.0	—	—	0.0	0.3	0.3	1.8	S	S	—	—	2.5	1.7	1.2	1.2
	200–999	S	S	0.3	0.2	0.0	0.1	0.5	0.5	4.4	5.7	0.6	0.8	0.2	3.3	2.4	2.6	1.9	2.5
	> 1,000	S	S	S	S	—	—	1.2	1.3	6.1	7.7	0.3	S	1.2	1.1	5.7	6.1	4.2	4.6
	total	S	S	0.8	0.9	0.6	0.5	1.1	1.2	5.4	6.9	0.4	0.7	1.2	1.2	5.3	5.6	3.9	4.3
Foreign-owned companies	< 200	S	S	—	—	—	—	S	S	—	—	S	S	—	—	0.0	0.5	0.0	0.2
	200–999	0.7	0.7	S	S	S	S	0.7	1.2	7.9	7.6	—	—	0.5	0.7	5.0	4.5	2.5	2.5
	> 1,000	S	S	—	—	—	—	—	—	0.7	0.8	—	—	—	—	4.3	4.1	2.9	2.9
	total	0.8	0.7	S	S	S	S	0.6	0.9	3.2	3.3	S	S	0.5	0.7	4.3	4.1	2.5	2.6
Swedish national companies	< 200	S	S	0.0	0.3	0.0	0.0	0.1	0.0	1.1	1.0	S	S	S	S	0.4	0.5	0.2	0.3
	200–999	0.3	0.3	0.2	0.3	0.1	0.1	0.1	0.1	1.2	4.1	1.2	1.6	0.1	0.1	1.1	1.2	0.6	0.8
	> 1,000	S	S	S	S	S	—	0.3	0.4	S	S	S	S	0.1	0.1	1.1	0.7	1.1	1.0
	total	1.2	0.6	0.1	0.3	0.1	0.1	0.2	0.2	2.2	3.4	2.4	3.0	0.1	0.1	1.0	1.0	0.7	0.8
Total		1.1	0.7	0.5	0.7	0.2	0.2	0.7	0.8	3.8	5.0	1.2	1.5	1.0	1.0	4.7	4.9	3.0	3.2

S = number of companies too small for publication.
Source: SOU (1982:15, p. 42).

R&D Activities in Swedish Subsidiaries Abroad

Information in this section about Swedish companies' R&D abroad has been extracted from DIRK's reports and also from a study carried out by the National Industry Board (SIND) which has been mentioned previously (SIND, 1980:4). The SIND study indicated that 43 out of a total of 118 Swedish multinationals conducted some form of R&D abroad in 1978. The research carried out by these groups outside Sweden corresponded to 11 per cent of industrial R&D in Sweden in 1978. This proportion can be compared with the number of employees in foreign subsidiaries in relation to total employment in industry in Sweden, which in 1978 was 25 per cent. R&D costs in the group of companies conducting R&D abroad amounted to an average of 16 per cent of the companies' total R&D budgets.

Thus, the R&D carried out by Swedish multinationals abroad is relatively less extensive than their foreign manufacturing operations. Furthermore, our study provides no evidence that this proportion has changed markedly. Despite the fact that the number of corporations conducting R&D abroad increased from 14 to 43 in the period 1965–78, the proportion of industry's total R&D operations abroad only increased slightly. The major share of this increase occurred in the period 1970–4, when research costs abroad increased more than the growth of production outside Sweden. The rise in research costs abroad was also greater than for the corresponding costs in Sweden. However, in the most recent period (1974–8), growth in R&D abroad has declined and was somewhat less than the increase in Sweden. One reason for this development is that some R&D intensive subsidiaries were disposed of in this period.

At a later stage in Chapter 9, we will show that the proportions of foreign sales and foreign production in Swedish multinationals increased in the period 1965–78. Since the proportion of R&D activities abroad did not increase simultaneously, the R&D intensity in the Swedish operations of these multinationals increased. Developments are indicated in Table 7.2 which shows that R&D activities in Sweden, in relation to sales in Sweden, increased more than for the corporate groups as a whole. Thus the expansion of production abroad has not involved any diminution of R&D activities in Sweden so far. On the contrary, the R&D intensity in Sweden has increased. This means that increased foreign manufacturing has, in many cases, been a precondition for increased sales which has made an expansion of R&D possible. This expansion has mainly taken place in Sweden.

There are considerable variations between companies as regards the localisation of R&D activities in Swedish multinationals. Thus, the ten largest investors have 30 per cent of their R&D abroad, while the average for the 43 companies with such activities was only 6 per cent. Table 7.3 indicates that the proportion of R&D activities abroad varies between industries. Thus, almost half of R&D activities abroad occur in subsidiaries in the engineering industry — this industry has almost 40 per cent of its R&D abroad. The two other industries with extensive R&D abroad are the chemical industry and the electrical products industry.

Table 7.2: R&D Intensity for Swedish Multinationals, 1965–78 (%)

	1965	1970	1974	1978
Total R&D/Total group turnover	1.84	2.15	2.22	2.30
Total R&D/Swedish company turnover	2.48	3.01	3.25	3.77
Swedish R&D/Swedish company turnover	2.27	2.53	2.77	3.23

Source: SOU (1982:27, p. 131).

Table 7.3: Distribution of R&D Costs in Sweden and Abroad in 1978

	R&D Costs		Distribution of		
	Sweden and Abroad (A)	Sweden only (B)	A as proportion of total for all industries	B/A (%)	(A − B)/B (%)
Food, beverages and tobacco	12	12	0	100	0
Textiles, clothing, leather goods	1	1	0	100	0
Paper and pulp	73	70	2	96	4
Paper products and printing	18	13	1	72	28
Chemicals, rubber, plastics	455	393	13	86	14
Iron, steel, metals	257	239	7	93	7
Metal goods	319	31	1	79	21
Machinery	667	426	19	64	36
Electrical goods	916	827	25	90	10
Vehicles and transport goods (incl. shipbuilding)	766	736	21	96	4
Other industries	82	77	2	94	6
Composite industries	335	282	9	84	16
All industries	3,621	3,109	100	86	14

Source: SOU (1982:27, p. 128)

Industries with a high proportion of their R&D abroad are also characterised by the highest level of R&D intensity in their foreign subsidiaries. However, in these industries, too, research costs in relation to the sales value of production are lower in the subsidiaries than in the Swedish parent company. In other words, relatively more research takes place in the Swedish companies in such groups. The difference is least in paper and pulp, machinery and in the vehicle and transport products industries. The foreign subsidiaries in these industries also have the highest export shares (i.e. they sell the highest proportion of their production outside the host country) (SIND, 1980:4, p. 138). The SIND study concludes that these two circumstances imply that a specialisation on the production side is matched by a corresponding specialisation of R&D.

The industrial and economic significance of corporate R&D abroad is determined, not only by its extent, but also by the type of R&D activities. Does the R&D carried out by Swedish foreign subsidiaries mainly consist of relatively simple product development or is it rather a question of more long-term research? Figures for industry as a whole indicate that there is no great difference in the type of R&D carried out in Sweden and in Swedish companies' foreign subsidiaries. SIND's study showed that almost half of the R&D in manufacturing foreign subsidiaries was linked to the improvement of existing products, while 40 per cent was related to new development and 10 per cent was for long-term research (SIND, 1980:4, p. 143). In 1977 the corresponding proportions for Swedish industry as a whole were 45 per cent, 50 per cent and 5 per cent.[4] It is not the case, however, that companies with overseas production generally have a certain proportion of advanced research located in subsidiaries. In fact most of the advanced research is conducted by a few, fully internationalised, companies.

R&D Activities in Foreign-Owned Companies in Sweden

We have already mentioned the fact that foreign-owned companies in Sweden are more R&D intensive than national companies but have relatively less R&D than the Swedish multinationals. Of the 57 foreign companies in our research population, 28 companies conducted R&D activities in 1977. The major proportion of these are former Swedish companies which were involved in R&D before their acquisition. However, newly formed foreign-owned companies also have considerable R&D in Sweden and are, in fact, the most R&D intensive of all companies studied.

Although the foreign-owned companies do not have as high an average R&D intensity as the Swedish multinationals, the foreign-owned corporations are more R&D intensive than Swedish subsidiaries abroad. One explanation may be that a considerable proportion of the foreign-owned companies were formerly domestic companies with R&D activities. Another explanation may be that Sweden, at least previously, was considered to be an interesting test market for consumer products since Sweden had a high standard of living and a pattern of consumption which was in advance of that achieved by most other European countries (Samuelsson, 1977). A third explanation might be that Sweden has had a relatively good supply of competent personnel and research staff. The fact that foreign corporations in the electrical and electronics industries have had the highest level of R&D intensity may be interpreted as support for this explanation. However, as mentioned, the concentration of R&D activities in the foreign-owned sector is high — three companies are responsible for roughly half of the R&D volume (SIND, 1980:4, p. 217). Since we do not have any additional information about these cases, we cannot draw any firm conclusions.

To summarise, we may note that the foreign-owned sector as a whole is more R&D intensive than Swedish national companies and Swedish subsidiaries abroad. Of the foreign companies, those established through greenfield investments are the most R&D intensive of all. Our study also attempted an investigation of what happened to R&D activities in companies, previously Swedish-owned, after the foreign takeover. This investigation proved to be problematical, however, due to weaknesses in the Swedish Central Bureau of Statistics' R&D figures. It was only possible to collect comparable valid data for 11 companies — two of the 11 showed increased R&D intensity after acquisition while nine showed reductions. If the R&D costs in all foreign-owned companies are totalled, it appears that this category did not reduce its proportion of R&D carried out in Swedish industry (SOU, 1982:19).

Finally, the R&D emphasis in the foreign-owned companies involved product development to a greater extent than for other categories of companies. More than 90 per cent of the R&D expenditure in the foreign companies in the period studied was devoted to product-oriented activities as compared with a proportion of 75 per cent in Swedish multinationals and 70 per cent in Swedish national companies.

Dissemination of New Technology and Know-How via Multinational Corporations

The proportion of Swedish exports attributable to Swedish multinational corporations was 58 per cent in 1978. This international trade is probably the most important way in which multinational companies spread technological know-how across national frontiers. It is more difficult to estimate how much technology was disseminated as a result of direct investments or the sale of licences. All we know, in fact, is that multinational companies represent an important element in the spread of technology, as can be seen in patenting and licensing agreements (see Table 7.4).

Table 7.4: Costs and Revenues: Licences and Patents in 1978

	Revenues from abroad		Costs paid abroad	
	Skr million	%	Skr million	%
Between independent companies	430	54.4	314	36.4
Within group of companies	361	45.6	550	63.7
Total	791	100.0	863	100.0
of which to/from foreign-owned companies	99	12.5	505	58.5

Source: SCB (1980:1).

Payments from Sweden to foreign countries for patents, licences and royalties have increased by 13 per cent per year since the mid 1960s. This is about the same rate of increase experienced by other West European countries. Commencing in 1977, the Swedish Central Bureau of Statistics distributed questionnaires to obtain more detailed data for foreign trade in services (SCB, 1978:7 and 1980:1).[5] These questionnaire surveys indicate that a very high proportion of payments for licences and patents takes place between companies belonging to the same corporate group. Groups of companies represented almost half the revenues and almost 60 per cent of the cost. Roughly the same proportions have been observed previously for other countries in an OECD report (1970).

Although multinational companies represent a large proportion of international licence payments, such payments do not amount to large sums in comparison with the volume of direct investments. We interpret this as meaning that the sale of licences is not primarily an alternative to direct investment, but is, rather, the result of direct investments.

Summary

Swedish groups with manufacturing operations abroad were responsible for 70 per cent of Swedish industry's R&D costs, foreign-owned companies for 5 per cent and national companies for 25 per cent. The multinational companies not only accounted for a greater volume of R&D but also had higher R&D intensity (i.e. more extensive R&D activities in relation to their size) than other companies. The multinationals have also increased their R&D intensity, while other categories have reduced R&D between 1973 and 1979. On the other hand there are no great differences between the categories of companies as regards the emphasis of R&D activities on long-term or short-term development. A closer analysis of the companies' R&D costs indicates that these vary considerably from industry to industry and also in accordance with the size of the company. R&D activity is greater in certain industries and is proportionally more for larger companies.

Even in Swedish multinationals with a high proportion of production abroad, R&D operations are mainly located in Sweden. Thus the 20 largest employers of personnel abroad conducted 86 per cent of their R&D activities in Sweden in 1978. The effects of direct investments have therefore influenced the volume of R&D activities in Sweden positively. However, certain extensively internationalised companies, especially those which manufacture machinery, have localised a substantial proportion of their R&D within foreign subsidiaries. Financial and business reasons have, in such cases, led to localisation within large, specialised subsidiaries. Where continued internationalisation leads to the location of R&D abroad, it is probable that the effects will be negative. But seen generally, the international sales of the Swedish multinational permitted them to undertake R&D activities on a much larger scale than would have been the case without these sales.

Notes

1. The corresponding proportion for the USA in 1966 was 52 per cent (US Tariff Commission, 1973, p. 557).

2. Three companies are responsible for approximately half of the total R&D in the foreign-owned companies category.

3. R&D intensity is measured here as total R&D in relation to group turnover in Sweden.

4. As previously mentioned, there was no substantial difference between the type of R&D in Swedish multinationals and other companies in Sweden.

5. The 1980 study was based on a sample of companies and the results are adjusted to cover Swedish industry as a whole.

8 INTERNATIONAL COMPETITIVENESS

We define competitiveness as the ability to maintain and develop positions on markets where sales take place in competition with other companies and other countries. The concept becomes easier to discuss if the level of wages is assumed to be given. We have assumed that success in international markets should not be primarily achieved by means of reductions in the level of wages but rather by increases in efficiency. Competitiveness then becomes an expression for efficiency in all functions of the company or the country. We apply the concept of competitiveness at three different levels: the group of companies as a whole, the Swedish companies in the group, and Swedish industry as a whole. This section covers competitiveness at the group and company-within-the-group level while the corresponding discussion which applies to Swedish industry as a whole is dealt with later in the chapter.

International investments are the result of decisions taken by individual companies. If we assume that companies will not take action that contradicts their ambition to maintain their competitive position, we should find that investments, at the time of the original decision, were considered likely to improve the company's competitive position, or at least to lead to greater competitiveness than if the investment had not taken place. Even if we do not anticipate that international investments, on an *a priori* basis, damage the companies' competitive position, it may be desirable to try to examine the relationship between foreign direct investments and competitiveness to assess how possible restrictions on direct investments influence competitiveness. It is therefore important to ask what factors constitute competitiveness. What is it that makes companies believe that foreign manufacturing is the most advantageous alternative and how strong are the reasons for such assessments in various cases?

We will first attempt to answer this question as it applies to Swedish multinational groups of companies by analysing the effect on competitiveness, taking the reasons given by companies for their investments as our starting point. In the majority of cases, investments took place to enable companies to maintain or expand their sales in a foreign market. In a smaller number of cases the primary motive was that foreign manufacturing appeared to be cheaper, or was to be preferred for other reasons. In both cases it appears that foreign investments were advantageous for reasons of profitability but it would not be particularly informative simply to analyse investments in terms of profit. This is particularly clear if we examine the effects on investment from a longer-term perspective and also attempt to estimate the total effect of all foreign investments made by a company.

After first describing the data relating to how direct investments influence the competitive position of Swedish multinational groups of companies in the long-term and in the short-term, we would like to consider the question of how the purely Swedish operations in such groups are affected. From the point of view of the Swedish company, it is clearly interesting to know whether international production contributes to strengthening competitiveness in all areas in the group or if only some sections of the group improve their positions to any greater extent. We include data referring to profitability and efficiency for all industrial companies in Sweden in order to illustrate this point. We can then compare the Swedish units of Swedish multinationals, the group of Swedish national companies, and foreign companies' subsidiaries in Sweden.

Competitiveness manifests itself at the group and company-within-the-group level in terms of efficiency (measured for example as profit), growth and market share. At the company-within-the-group level, the use of such measuring instruments is somewhat dubious and therefore we also include a factor termed the localisation of 'functions for the development of competitiveness' (R&D, management, manufacture of key components for the product system and central marketing) to provide support for statements about competitiveness.

The Effect of Direct Investments on the Competitiveness of Groups of Companies in the Short Term

According to international investment theory, it is assumed that a company making a foreign investment possesses a competitive advantage which enables the company to sell profitably on a foreign market. However, if one company is to manufacture products abroad, there must, in addition, be one or more external factors or conditions which justify such investment — otherwise the company would have exported from the home country.

There are several external factors which may contribute to making the establishment of foreign operations a more advantageous alternative to manufacturing in the home country and exports. The first group of factors involves various barriers to trade which may be natural — for example long distances which give rise to high transport costs — or they may be artificial, such as tariffs or quantitative restrictions designed to hinder imports and favour domestic production. If barriers to trade are the main reason for the establishment of foreign production operations, we speak of so-called 'market-oriented investments'. In such cases local manufacturing is one way of circumventing or bridging trade barriers and thus permits the company to achieve higher sales than would otherwise have been the case. Manufacturing costs, however, do not necessarily need to be lower on the foreign market.

A second group of external factors which may justify foreign manufacturing involves items which determine conditions for production in various ways. It may be ease of access to raw materials, or expert knowledge which is essential for production operations; alternatively, low wage costs or company subsidies may permit lower prices or higher profits than would otherwise have been possible. Where one or more of these factors have been largely decisive, we speak of 'resource-oriented investments'. In practice, it may well be difficult to find pure cases of either of these two types of investment. It is, however, generally possible to state which type of reasoning has been dominant. The majority of foreign investments by Swedish companies were market-oriented. This applies both when new companies have been established and when existing companies have been purchased. We will therefore consider market-oriented situations first, to be followed by the few cases of resource-oriented investments which have been studied.

Market-Oriented Investments

Our investigations indicate that artificial barriers to trade were an important factor in the early establishment of many Swedish engineering companies abroad. In some cases, the host country required manufacture of the product in the country in question. This was the case for the Ericsson group of companies and their foreign competitors in the telecommunications industry. As a rule, the purchasers (i.e. the telephone and telegraph administrations in the various countries) are obliged to take certain criteria into account which are not purely technical or financial. The choice of supplier is not only determined on the basis of the technical quality of the products, but is also influenced by whether the supplier manufactures the products within the country's borders, to a greater or lesser extent. The local manufacturing criteria have resulted in the production of a major proportion of such equipment designed for the public network within the user country.

As a result, local manufacturing companies have been considered essential in the competitive situation faced by Ericsson. Without such foreign companies, sales to public administrations, which are Ericsson's major customers, would not have taken place in many cases. It is not, however, impossible that licences could have been sold, together with some exports from Sweden for a brief period following the introduction of a new, superior product by Ericsson. But over a longer period of time local presence has been the most important competitive advantage.

The situation for the telecommunications industry is not unique. For example, in the market of rock drills and drilling equipment, practically all markets outside Europe have some form of protection against imports. One explanation of this situation is that the mining industry, an important customer, is under some form of government control in most countries. Each country had its own standardisation norms which *de facto* give local manufacturers a competitive advantage over foreign producers. Certain countries, such as France, even specify that rock drills must be manufactured locally.

The fact that this type of trade barrier has been so significant for the Swedish engineering industry can be partly explained by the type of products sold by engineering companies. The products involve high technology, and large orders, and are sold to public buyers or to buyers who cannot ignore the issue of 'public interest'. This buyer structure has probably been advantageous for the relatively small Swedish companies with limited sales resources but it has also meant that companies have been forced to locate manufacturing abroad to a greater extent than would have been justified by transport and production costs alone.

ESAB, which manufactures welding products, can be seen as an example of a company where a combination of artificial and natural trade barriers have led to the decision to set up manufacturing facilities in France. For the first two decades after the establishment of the French plant, manufacturing within the EEC customs union meant that ESAB was able to use price to a greater extent than would otherwise have been possible in order to win over certain customers. For certain buyers, such as defence ministries, it has also been important that the supplier had domestic manufacturing operations. Furthermore, local production made it easier for ESAB to manufacture special product variants for certain major customers, and direct contacts between the buyer and manufacturing operations facilitated product development. A short distance between the manufacturer and the buyer is advantageous in this industry, since transport costs are relatively high in relation to the price of the product and manufacturing economies of scale are not very significant.

Our studies of the welding industry and also of the ventilation industry have shown that companies in these fields would not actually have been expected to undertake direct investments. The reason for this opinion is that it is difficult for a company to achieve a competitive advantage which is specific for the company. Previously, the products and the production processes were relatively standardised. Furthermore, there are many buyers and they are widely dispersed. Trade-mark strategies can only be used to a certain extent, but the fact that there is a large number of competitors means that the price is inevitably a vital competitive tool. The reason why these companies could move abroad, despite all the difficulties, is that there must have been certain advantages associated with size and that ESAB and Fläkt were successful in establishing long-standing relationships with buyers and distribution channels. The companies did not originally have these advantages, however — they were the result of foreign activities. Thus we have found cases which are not in agreement with the eclectic theory of foreign direct investment theory which states that companies which establish operations abroad already have an advantage which is specific to that company. When we transfer our attention to the study of direct investments which have taken place via an acquisition purchase of foreign companies, it becomes even more clear that certain cases of establishment abroad have been a method designed to achieve an advantage rather than a way of exploiting an existing advantage.

An increasing proportion of cases where foreign companies are set up has taken the form of the purchase of existing foreign companies (see Table 3.7). Our studies of individual establishments of operations abroad show that the major share of these company purchases has taken place to achieve a rapid increase in sales on a foreign market or to defend a position which has already been won, where the Swedish company was already previously represented on the market.

In some cases an important reason for purchasing has been that the parent company wished to introduce new technology or new product know-how into the organisation. Irrespective of which reasons have been the most important, the parent company has taken the view that the acquisition of a foreign company was either cheaper or less risky or both than the corresponding commencement of a new operation.

There may be several reasons why the purchase of a company is considered to be cheaper than setting up a new company. The fact that an existing company's market value is lower than the realisable value of its assets may be because prices for the company's products have not increased as rapidly as the prices of investment goods (capital goods). It may also be the case that the owners of the existing company fear increased competition if they do not sell and if the foreign company chooses to establish itself on the local market. If demand on the market does not increase sufficiently rapidly, increased competition means lower profitability for the existing companies. By selling the company to the foreign buyer, the owners can achieve a price which is higher than the company's value in a tougher competitive situation. For the buyer, on the other hand, the purchase price will be lower than the equivalent green-field investment.

The short-term effects of a company purchase on competitiveness may therefore primarily be that profitability can be improved and total sales increased. However, the long-term effects are more important — the company achieves a stronger market position. This point is further discussed below.

Resource-Oriented Investments

Important sectors of Swedish industry have been traditionally based on domestic raw materials. This may explain why the foreign investments made by Swedish companies are so little resource-oriented. In countries with a limited raw materials base, such as Japan and Great Britain, a considerable proportion of the outflow of direct investments can be characterised as resource-oriented. In the case of Sweden, we can find examples of such resource-oriented investments in only one industry, the clothing industry. The establishment of manufacturing operations abroad by the Swedish clothing industry should be seen against a background of considerable increases in imports of clothing which drove large sectors of the Swedish clothing industry out of business in the 1960s and 1970s. Increased imports were, amongst other things, the result of lower manufacturing costs and thus of lower prices offered by foreign competitors. The reduction or removal of tariffs and the growth of large retail chains in Sweden were other important conditions favouring im-ports. The new retail chains, with active purchase departments, looked about for foreign supplies, thus facing the Swedish manufacturers with increased competition.

The Swedish clothing industry tried to meet competition from im-ports by reducing production costs, but failed. In order to reduce total manufacturing costs, manufacturing operations were transferred abroad. The Swedish clothing companies invested in their own facilities in Europe and made use of subcontracting to some extent. This contributed to some improvement in the competitive position of these companies, even if it was marginal. In fact, the difficulties experienced by the Swedish clothing industry were not just due to high manufacturing costs. There were also deficiencies in design, trade-mark strategies and other factors. The fact that a considerable proportion of imports of clothing into Sweden comes from countries with not particularly low wages can be seen as evidence of these deficiencies. Costs for sewing clothes, the production operation which has been most often located abroad, represent only a small proportion of the total manufacturing costs. In addition, certain types of clothing consumption are not particularly price sensitive and therefore there are opportunities for companies with high manufacturing costs if they make the 'right' products.

The Effect of Direct Investments on the Competitiveness of Groups of Companies in the Long Term

The major Swedish multinationals in the engineering industry have at least one factor in common — they acquired technological know-how which other companies did not have at a very early stage. What distinguishes technological know-how from other types of assets in a company is that it does not decline in value when it is exploited, since it is neither damaged nor worn out. Technology used on one market can be applied on other markets without any appreciable additional costs. It was therefore more profitable to expand and to sell unique products on foreign markets than to develop new know-how for new areas of activity in Sweden.

The engineering companies' increased foreign sales provided a financial surplus which was used both for product development, leading to a higher quality and wider range of products, and for the creation of a network of marketing and warehousing subsidiaries in various countries. Market investments for these Swedish companies, mainly selling producer goods with other companies as buyers, meant that they built up close and long-lasting relationships with their customers involving mutual dependence between supplier and customer. This made it easier for the Swedish companies to comply with the wishes of foreign buyers and it was also more difficult for competitors to win over these buyers to their products.

As time went on, these investments in marketing had become so important that, in many cases, it would be quite justified to regard the relationships between buyers and the established marketing and service network as the Swedish engineering companies' main competitive tool. Sometimes it has not been possible to maintain the early technological advantage on the product side, since technological development activities offered diminishing returns and competitors have successively increased their stock of know-how.

As already mentioned, the next stage in the internationalisation of companies has taken the form of local manufacturing in order to counteract trade barriers. Thus, the prime motivation has not been lower costs for labour, since lower costs have usually been counteracted by lower productivity and it would, instead, be more appropriate to speak of marketing investments in the production phase. Generally speaking, the final phase in the manufacturing process, involving product adaptation or assembly, has been the prime target for transfer abroad. Local manufacturing has then been slowly extended to achieve a wider coverage of production processes.

A growing proportion of foreign investments in the 1970s, above all in industries which had a high level of company concentration, consisted of the acquisition of existing companies. Large companies prefer to buy out the remaining competitors rather than eliminate them through competition. Seen against a background of a somewhat longer time perspective, the purchase of competitors leads to further advantages in the form of increased total sales and higher market shares. Although efficiency may increase as a result of a larger scale of operations, this is not a major factor. The parent company's access to a market network with established customer relationships is more important. In the case of vertically integrated industries, the purchase of other companies can be a method of ensuring continued sales and may provide opportunities for better production planning. When, for example, ASSI acquired some of its previous customers in the paper sack and corrugated cardboard industries in Great Britain, the company gained control of more stages in the manufacturing chain.

We may also suspect, on good grounds, that multinationals may wish to protect their positions, as can be seen in, for example, the Electrolux acquisition of the American vacuum cleaner manufacturer, Nation Union Electric (NUE) and Sandvik's purchase of the French rock-drill manufacturer, Le Burin. When a local company comes up for sale, for any reason, there are often purchasers ready and waiting amongst the other companies in the industry. What decides who becomes the buyer is then partly a question of who has the largest capital resources, and who has most to gain by increasing market shares or most to lose if another company increases its market share. In the Electrolux case, American antitrust legislation prevented American companies from buying NUE — and this was, of course, a considerable advantage for Electrolux.

In the final phase of the internationalisation process, the multinational company allows its subsidiaries or independent subcontractors to specialise in certain areas of the organisation's product range and sell such specialised products to markets outside the host country. Previously, SKF's foreign subsidiaries manufactured the major proportion of the group's product range for local market sales. Only the Swedish SKF companies could report exports of any significance. Commencing in 1978, SKF have developed a new structure which means that approximately half of the European manufacturing companies' production is sold locally while the other half is exported to other subsidiaries in Europe (*Euromoney*, September 1982). Similarly, Fläkt's French and Belgian subsidiaries have specialised in the manufacture of fans and heat-exchangers, respectively. The EEC customs union has been a prerequisite for this product specialisation on the part of subsidiaries.

This description of the development process lying behind the internationalisation of Swedish companies provides some information which is essential for an assessment of the relationship between international investments and competitiveness. Foreign investments may thus be both a method of exploiting an existing competitive advantage and an opportunity to gain new advantages. When competitiveness is based on technological superiority, the driving force behind foreign investments is to exploit this superiority. In situations where technological superiority is of no great significance, it appears that opportunities to improve market position or to acquire technology seem to be important reasons for the establishment of production facilities abroad.

The Effects of Outward Direct Investments on the Competitiveness of the Swedish Parts of the Groups

It is far from obvious that the competitive advantages which follow from direct investments, directly or indirectly, favour all units in the organisations concerned. In certain conditions, industrial development in the parent company has been boosted, while, in other cases, foreign manufacturing may lead to a weakening of the parent company's position. In the case of a country where investments across its frontiers are in balance and where the pattern of industry is roughly similar for investment inflows and outflows, it may not matter much whether competitiveness increases in the parent company or in the subsidiaries. Losses from investment flows abroad are regained in investment inflows and vice versa. However, from the Swedish point of view, where investment outflows

are considerably higher than the inflows, it would, of course, have been
an advantage if international expansion had primarily increased the competitiveness of the parent company. For obvious reasons, it is difficult
to assess empirically that this is the case. We can make a start by presenting information gained in the case and industrial sector studies and
describe what could be characterised as well-founded hypotheses about
what happens to competitiveness in the Swedish units of multinational
companies. The next step is to illustrate the development of efficiency
in the Swedish elements of the company groups using information from
Swedish industrial statistics. This information does not apply, however,
to different parts of the same group but is, instead, a comparison between the categories of Swedish multinational companies' Swedish units,
foreign companies and national companies which were used previously.

Whether foreign direct investments lead to strengthened competitiveness for the parent company or not depends, for example, on
which production operations are performed abroad and in the home
country. Studies of Swedish foreign investments by industry have indicated that, generally speaking, the simpler areas of the production process have been located abroad while the advanced phases of production,
based on technological leads, have been retained and developed further
in Sweden. The situation at Sandvik is a good illustration of this. Sandvik's production of rock drills can be divided up into four stages: (i)
manufacture of drill steel; (ii) production of cemented carbide powder;
(iii) manufacture of cemented carbide cutting edges; (iv) assembly of
rock drills. The foreign subsidiaries originally started as assembly factories. The number of production stages carried out abroad has then been
progressively increased and the production range extended. The rate at
which subsidiaries with manufacturing operations have been given increased production responsibility has depended on the growth and profitability of the local foreign market. Figure 8.1 shows the proportion
of production in the various stages carried out in Sweden and at Sandvik's foreign facilities. Sandvik is one of the few companies in the world
manufacturing drill steel and all manufacturing is still retained in Sweden.
In the second production stage too, the manufacture of cemented carbide powder, all production should be located in Sweden if profitability
were the only relevant measure. The profitability limit for the manufacture of cemented carbide powder, according to Sandvik's estimate, is
around 300 tonnes. 125 tonnes are produced in India, 100 tonnes in South
Africa, 130 tonnes in Brazil and 360 tonnes in Britain; 1,700 tonnes are
manufactured in Sweden, of which 600 tonnes are exported to foreign
subsidiaries.

Figure 8.1: Proportion of Sandvik's Production of Rock Drills in Sweden and Abroad

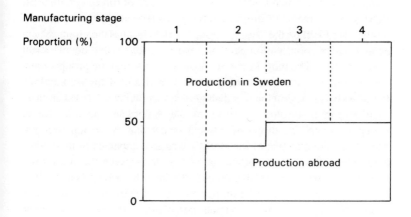

Source: Sandvik.

Our case studies indicate that the parent company's competitive position is strengthened most when the activities of subsidiaries are closely integrated with those of the parent company. This is the case with vertical integration where the parent company invests in a subsequent production stage abroad. ASSI's purchase of paper sack and corrugated cardboard companies and Electrolux's purchase of Arthur Martin in France can be seen as examples of such vertically integrated moves. In both cases the parent company's competitive ability was improved, since the parent gained better control over sales channels and better contact with the market.

In the clothing industry, the purpose of setting up companies abroad was not to come closer to the market but rather to cut manufacturing costs. The aspect of manufacturing which was relocated was the actual function of sewing clothes while other functions such as design, purchasing, the production of samples, the acquisition of capital, etc., were retained in Sweden. The combination of domestic and foreign manufacturing has enabled a company such as Janstorp to survive in a price-sensitive segment of the market subject to competitive imports. Although the expansion of foreign manufacturing has been paralleled by a decline in production in Sweden, we would draw the conclusion that Swedish competitiveness would have been even weaker if Janstorp had not established itself abroad.

When a foreign subsidiary carries out activities in parallel with the parent company, it is not quite as clear that it is the parent company's competitiveness which is strengthened as a result of foreign operations. PLM's investments in European glassworks have not led to a dominant position for PLM on the West European market, nor has the group achieved any major coordination gains as regards research and development or purchasing. The most important result has been that the group's competitive position has been strengthened as a result of higher yields in the subsidiaries and in the Swedish glassworks divisions. In other cases such as the Electrolux purchase of the American vacuum cleaner manufacturer NUE, direct investment meant that the group strengthened its position as one of the world's largest companies in its product area. Thus, the investment can be said to have given the group as a whole increased opportunities to claim monopoly profits as a result of its stronger position in relation to competitors. Finally, in a situation where the foreign subsidiary pursues completely independent activities, the parent company cannot strengthen its position through market dominance and integration gains. In this case, it is primarily the financial yield achieved by the subsidiary which can assist the parent company.

These examples suggest that the importance of foreign production for the competitive position of the Swedish units in multinational groups depends on how foreign manufacturing is integrated into the parent company's activities and how large and how independent the subsidiaries are. Thus, the most positive effect that can be anticipated would occur in cases where the foreign subsidiary is responsible for the final, less complicated stages of the manufacturing process if sales advantages not possible via exports are also achieved. Possible negative effects occur when the foreign subsidiary is given central responsibility within the group for the manufacture and development of certain products. This has only happened in a few cases, as far as we know, but the probability of further cases occurring is increasing as multinational groups become more internationalised.

The conclusion from the cases is thus that the internationalisation which has taken place hitherto in the production area seems to have had largely positive effects on activities in Sweden. Companies have maintained their position on the world market, while expanding most of the functions which develop the group's competitiveness in Sweden. The question is whether this tendency can also be traced in the statistics describing profitability for categories of companies as a whole.

Foreign studies have showed that foreign-owned companies have higher productivity than domestically-owned companies (Dunning, 1958;

Information Canada, 1970; Jungnickel *et al.*, 1977; Parry, 1978; Reuber *et al.*, 1973; Van den Bulcke and Halsberghe, 1979). Parry (1980) maintains that the higher productivity achieved by foreign-owned companies may depend on factors such as technological advantages, economies of scale in the manufacture of components, better management and greater financial resources. A further explanation might be that they are able to purchase components and raw materials more cheaply. Dunning (1958) compares productivity in American subsidiaries in Britain with productivity in the parent companies. He shows that the subsidiaries have lower productivity and explains this in terms of the subsidiaries' inability to mechanise manufacturing to the same degree as a result of the small scale of activities and the fact that the subsidiaries had an excessively large product range in relation to the size of the market.

Previous studies of profitability in multinational companies have provided that foreign-owned companies have higher profitability than the corresponding domestic companies. Several studies have indicated this — for example Samuelsson (1977) in a study covering 1970. In this study, the difference between the foreign and domestic companies' profitability was greatest in the engineering and chemical industries. SIND's study of the food industry also found that foreign-owned companies achieved higher profits than the industry average (SIND, 1977:10).

Unfortunately, there are no corresponding studies of the profitability of the multinational parent companies in relation to domestic companies in the home country. What has been analysed in some studies is the profitability of multinational groups. Furthermore, the results are not unambiguous. Some reported that multinationals achieve higher profits than other companies, while Rugman (1981) found that US multinationals earned just normal profits (Vaupel, 1971; Dunning and Pearce, 1981). In terms of the theory of internalisation this absence of excess profits would mean that the costs of running the internal market offset any monopolistic firm-specific advantage of the multinational company.

Some reworking of the financial data by the Swedish Central Bureau of Statistics has made it possible to compare the profitability of the activities of Swedish multinational companies in Sweden, Swedish national companies, foreign-owned companies in Sweden and Swedish companies which are partially foreign-owned. Profitability comparisons between companies are hazardous for a number of reasons. The first point is that companies should be comparable so that systematic discrepancies between categories, as regards the industry involved and size, do not lie behind differences in profit. Furthermore, the profit and profitability measures used emanate from the companies themselves. Since companies are able, within a fairly wide framework, to distribute profits between various operational years, the balance sheet presentations do not always give a true picture of real differences in profitability. Furthermore, where internationally active companies are concerned, it is difficult to determine how profits should be split between activities in various countries. Finally, companies which are expanding rapidly often return lower profits than companies in stagnation, since the expanding enterprise is progressively investing in new plants and is entitled to larger deductions for depreciation.

With these reservations in mind, we may note that the foreign-owned group of companies have the highest profitability of all the categories studied. Table 8.1 shows profitability in terms of yield on equity capital. In the period studied, the foreign-owned companies increased their lead in profitability and even improved on profits achieved in what are termed 'the excess profit years' (i.e. the boom which followed the oil-price shock in 1973). A comparison was made between subsidiaries that had been purchased and subsidiaries started from scratch to see if the foreign-owned companies' high profitability could be explained as a result of their purchase of especially profitable Swedish companies. It appeared, however, that the subsidiaries established through greenfield investments had just as high a profitability as those purchased and thus the high average figures for the foreign-owned company category do not account for the high profitability of previously Swedish-owned companies. Table 8.1 also indicates that national companies have experienced lower profitability than the Swedish multinationals. The largest national companies quite clearly had the least satisfactory development in terms of profit. When compared on an industry basis, there are still differences in profitability between categories, but these differences are reduced (SOU, 1982:15, p. 63).

Thus the figures for the profitability of the various categories do not lead us to reject the hypothesis of a correlation between multinationalism and profitability. Differences in profitability are, however, not great, especially not between the Swedish companies in Swedish-owned multinationals and other Swedish-owned corporations. Another explanation of the difficulty in tracing multinational superiority in profits could be that foreign investments do not affect the parent companies' profitability to any great extent. An alternative, and more likely, interpretation is that these companies invest resources more than other companies so as to strengthen their positions and that they invest large sums in research and development activities and sales organisations. Such expenses are booked as costs and have an immediate effect on profits, in contrast to

Table 8.1: Return on Equity for Categories of Companies in 1966–72 and 1973–7, (weighted average)

Size	Category	1966	1968	1970	1972	1973	1975	1977
200–999 Employees	Swedish multinational*	5.1	4.5	2.4	4.8	7.3	7.4	7.6
	Foreign-owned	6.1	9.8	9.7	9.7	14.7	13.5	16.3
	Foreign minority-owned	5.8	8.9	7.8	9.1	12.2	7.0	14.3
	Swedish national	4.4	4.6	5.5	5.6	10.1	4.4	8.6
Over 1,000 Employees	Swedish multinational*	5.6	6.7	7.0	5.5	9.2	9.1	4.9
	Foreign-owned	9.7	8.7	2.8	5.5	14.9	14.9	24.3
	Foreign minority-owned	4.0	10.2	4.2	5.2	11.8	1.5	14.2
	Swedish national	-0.3	-0.2	1.9	3.0	8.4	4.9	-7.1
Total	Swedish multinational*	5.6	6.5	6.9	5.5	9.0	8.9	5.2
	Foreign-owned	8.2	9.6	7.5	7.9	14.0	13.7	18.9
	Foreign minority-owned	4.2	10.0	7.1	7.9	12.1	5.9	15.8
	Swedish national	2.1	2.3	4.2	4.5	9.7	5.8	1.4
	Total population	4.9	5.7	6.4	5.4	9.5	7.4	5.4

*Includes activities in Sweden only.
Source: SOU (1982:5).

investments in physical assets. One hypothesis could thus be that multinationals do not choose to demonstrate the results of their stronger competitive position in the form of higher profitability but, rather, spend some of their resources to create a more secure position in the market. Such behaviour would reflect the fact that multinationals are large companies and are what is known as management-controlled, while the national, and often smaller, companies are more likely to be owner-controlled.

Summary

Trade barriers, whether natural or artificial, played an important part in the early establishments of foreign operations undertaken by many Swedish engineering companies. Trade barriers meant that companies were forced to locate more manufacturing abroad than would have been justified simply by transport and production costs, in order to maintain and expand foreign sales. The type of products sold by these companies offers a partial explanation as to why this type of trade barrier has been so significant for decisions relating to direct investments. High-technology products, sold to public buyers or to buyers who valued proximity to the source of production, were often involved.

An increasing proportion of foreign investments have taken place, chiefly in the last ten years, in the form of the acquisition of existing foreign companies. Most of these company purchases have taken place because that was one way to increase sales on a foreign market, or to protect a position already achieved if the Swedish company was already represented on the market. In some of the cases studied, an important reason for purchasing a company has been that the parent company wished to introduce new technology or new product know-how into the organisation. The purchase of companies has been predominantly positive for the competitiveness of the buyer, primarily because the groups involved have achieved a stronger position on the market.

Foreign investments primarily designed to exploit lower production costs abroad have mainly occurred in the clothing industry. Where clothing manufacturers could not switch production into less price-sensitive products, the alternative was to locate some of the sewing operations abroad. Clothing companies invested in their own plants in Europe and also made some use of contract manufacturers (not a direct investment but with similar effects).

We find that foreign investments can be both a method of exploiting an existing competitive advantage and a method of gaining an advantage. Direct investments have mainly strengthened the Swedish companies' competitive position where the subsidiaries' activities have been integrated with those of the parent companies. In many cases, foreign investments have led to the location of the simpler phases in the production process abroad, while the most sophisticated phases, based on technological leadership, have been retained and further developed in Sweden. Where the parent company has invested in one of the later production phases, competitive capability has improved as a result of increased control over sales operations and better contact with the market. Where the foreign subsidiary has been given principal responsibility within the group for the manufacture and development of certain products, the competitiveness of Swedish companies within the group may be negatively affected.

The foreign-owned category of companies has experienced the highest profitability and the best growth of profitability in the period studied. Within this group of foreign-owned companies, newly established companies had the same profitability as those that had been purchased and it is not, therefore, the previous high levels of profitability achieved by the original Swedish owners which have raised the average figure. National companies have had lower profitability than the Swedish units of Swedish multinationals for many years. Furthermore, the figures for multinationals may well be underestimated since multinationals invest more heavily in research and development and marketing, which are not booked as assets but treated as costs and charged against profit figures directly.

The Swedish multinationals have been successful in expanding and maintaining their position on the world market for many years. For the group as a whole, this situation is the ultimate criterion of competitiveness. In these expanding groups of companies, vital corporate functions and production phases have generally been retained in Sweden, which appears to be an indication that the Swedish units in such multinational groups have strengthened their positions.

9 EXPORTS

The significance of direct investments for exports and employment has been of central interest in studies carried out in other countries. The effects of foreign investments on exports and on employment are usually linked, since if a direct investment results in the manufacture of goods abroad rather than in the home country, this is assumed to create parallel effects, both in the home country's exports and on its employment figures. A failure to export does not necessarily involve increased unemployment in the home country if there is a shortage of the labour that would have been required for the production of such exports. We return to this question in the next chapter which discusses employment effects.

The effect of direct investments on Swedish exports will be illustrated in two ways. First, statistics are presented which demonstrate various correlations between exports and foreign investments. What does the link with exports look like in markets with appreciable Swedish foreign investments and in markets where such investments have been limited? What is the proportion of exports in companies with considerable foreign production or minimal foreign manufacturing? This statistical account does not attempt any causal analysis but is, rather, a description of how Swedish exports develop when companies internationalise their production. In order to make any statement about what would have happened to exports if direct investments had not taken place, we must look at individual companies, taking into account the conditions that have applied for each investment decision. The effect of foreign investments on exports have thus been analysed (Bergsten *et al.*, 1978, p. 213) in terms of two questions:

(i) To what extent would it have been possible to achieve current foreign sales of finished products purely on the basis of exports, without local production?

(ii) What has been the volume of exports of input components used in foreign production resulting directly from the establishment of foreign manufacturing facilities?

When dealing with the first question, effects are estimated by comparing actual exports through the foreign subsidiary with the hypothetical

110

alternative of addditional manufacture of the same product in Sweden, followed by export sales. This assumption may lead to an overestimation of the positive export effects of direct investments or an underestimate of the negative effects since, if some foreign manufacturing had not taken place, the company would probably have been able to find better alternatives than simply achieving modest exports or completely rejecting the export market in question. On the other hand, it is also possible that the alternative export opportunities are overestimated in certain cases. An example here might be where a company with a unique product establishes manufacturing abroad because it is not possible to recruit sufficient competent and skilled employees for increased manufacturing in Sweden. If we ignore the shortage of skilled personnel but look exclusively at the product's position on the market, it is possible to overestimate the export opportunities.

Thus, rather detailed studies of the individual companies' situation are required if we are to express an opinion about companies' export opportunities. Fortunately, case and industrial sector studies have frequently been successful in revealing the circumstances which applied at the time of the investment decision which argued against the export alternative. It is more difficult to assess what are the more long-term export efects since there are a great many other factors, apart from direct investments, which are relevant. An attempt can be made to trace more long-term effects in information about export developments for the whole group of multinational companies. Thus, we are now back with the type of broad correlation descriptions which have been mentioned previously and which will now be described.

Do Multinationals Export More than Other Companies?

The statistics which follow are intended to illustrate two questions. The first is whether multinationals export more or less than other companies. The second question is whether the production of Swedish multinationals abroad means a limitation on exports from Sweden. Before we can discuss these questions, the concepts used for exports and foreign sales must be defined. Exports, here, means sales abroad of products manufactured in Sweden. Such export sales may go to foreign customers or to the subsidiaries of Swedish companies abroad. The concept of foreign sales describes the total sales abroad of Swedish companies. Total foreign sales thus include both the sales value of products manufactured in Sweden for exports and the value of products manufactured by foreign production units. Economic interest is thus centred on how exports develop and on how the relationship between exports and foreign sales changes when foreign production expands.

The results of the various studies indicate clearly that the multinationals increased their exports more than the rest of Swedish industry. Companies with foreign manufacturing throughout the entire period 1965–78 increased their share of total Swedish exports from 40 per cent to 46 per cent. These companies' share of total employment in industry was 32 per cent in 1965 and 37 per cent in 1978. If we also include companies which established foreign manufacturing facilities in the period 1965–78, the multinationals' share of Swedish exports was 58 per cent (see Table 9.1). More than 60 per cent of the multinationals' exports originate with the twenty companies who had the most employees abroad.

Table 9.1: Total Swedish Exports, Exports from All Groups with Foreign Investments and from the 20 Largest Groups with Investments Abroad, 1965–78 (Skr million).

	1965	1970	1974	1978
Total Swedish exports	20,540	35,150	70,510	98,210
Exports by Swedish group companies,	8,500	19,500	38,100	56,700
as percentage of total exports	41	55	54	58
Exports from Swedish group companies representing the 20 largest foreign investors	5,550	11,730	22,740	35,600
as percentage of total exports	27	33	32	36

Source: SOU (1982:27).

The strong export position of the Swedish multinationals is also demonstrated by Table 9.2 which shows that their export intensity, measured as a ratio of exports to production value, is higher than for other company categories. The table also shows that export intensity varies very considerably between one industry and another and that this applies whether the companies are multinationals or not. In five of eight industries, the multinationals have higher export shares than the purely national companies. In two industries the proportions are roughly equal and in the non-metalliferous mining industry (ISIC 36) the national companies have a higher export share.

Table 9.2 also indicates that foreign-owned companies in Sweden

Table 9.2: Export Intensity for Various Company Categories (exports as a proportion of own production (%), by Industry, 1979, weighted average)

	Swedish Multi-nationals	Foreign-owned companies	Swedish national companies	Total all companies
ISIC 31	14	8	3	5
ISIC 32	39	60	40	42
ISIC 33	27	16	23	24
ISIC 34	63	37	39	53
ISIC 35	51	26	32	38
ISIC 36	22	28	26	24
ISIC 37	49	63	50	51
ISIC 38	70	57	42	65
ISIC 3	62	38	25	46

Source: SOU (1982:15).

had an export intensity of 38 per cent, a higher proportion than that achieved by national companies or by Swedish subsidiaries abroad (25 per cent). Other studies have found that foreign-owned subsidiaries in West Germany had an export intensity of 16 per cent in 1974, while in Canada the corresponding figure was 28 per cent in 1969. It appears, therefore, that the foreign-owned companies in Sweden have a relatively high export intensity, while the Swedish subsidiaries abroad are closer to the average achieved by foreign-owned companies in Canada and West Germany. Samuelsson's study of foreign-owned companies (1977) explains the high export shares (especially for North American companies) in terms of the availability of skilled workers in Sweden which made it advantageous to manufacture capital goods, not only for the local market but also for exports.

The foreign-owned companies in Sweden ship more than half of their exports to other companies within the same group. If the companies are divided up in terms of country of origin, we find that all foreign-owned corporations, except those based in West Germany, increased their exports to group companies. The West German figures, however, were already at a high level. North American companies in Sweden were responsible for the bulk of exports from foreign-owned companies and they doubled the proportion of their production shipped to group companies in the period 1975–7.

So far, in our description of the development of exports for the various company categories, we have assumed that more exports are better than fewer exports and that all figures about exports are directly comparable. Reality is not so simple, however. It may be questioned, for example, whether the import content in goods which are exported by various companies is roughly of the same proportion. If this is not the case, it is not possible to state that a company with higher exports than another company also makes a more positive contribution towards the country's balance of trade. An attempt was therefore made in the study of industrial sectors to estimate import intensity for the various company categories. Since it was only possible to distinguish imported goods which went directly to industrial companies, the estimates were, however, uncertain. It is, for example, likely that foreign-owned companies are less dependent on agents, traders and other intermediaries in Sweden than the Swedish companies and therefore foreign-owned companies appear in the statistics to a greater degree as importers. The results of the studies showed that the foreign-owned companies had the greatest import intensity and showed a negative trade balance *vis-à-vis* foreign countries. Multinationals and national companies had roughly the same proportion of imported goods in their production but, since the multinationals sold a higher proportion of their production in the form of exports, multinationals attained a more positive 'balance of trade', relatively speaking.

Studies of foreign-owned companies in Canada have shown that these foreign-owned companies often have a subordinate role in their respective groups. The development opportunities of subsidiaries are limited by restrictions on their right to export, to expand their product ranges and to conduct development activities. Where such restrictions are applied to Swedish companies which are acquired by foreign interests, negative effects on exports, for example, may occur. Where foreign companies invest in Sweden and build up new operations, the situation is different. In the long term, the balance of trade and unemployment can be improved if the establishment of manufacturing facilities leads to a drop in imports or an increase in exports. In order to determine whether the long-term effects are positive or not, we have to take into account, for example, whether such an establishment of manufacturing facilities influences the existing company structure. In the worst possible case, it may be that existing Swedish companies go to the wall as a result of the establishment of manufacturing facilities in Sweden by a foreign company and the foreign-owned company then produces purely for the Swedish market.

The case studies of four Swedish companies taken over by foreign

interests showed that there were considerable differences in the independent status of subsidiaries as regards questions such as export expansion. Findus is part of the Nestlé group, where it is company policy that
each subsidiary should chiefly supply its own home market. It is therefore
not improbable that exports from Findus would have developed more
positively if the company had remained in Swedish ownership. The problems experienced by the tyre manufacturer, Firestone-Viskafors, might
possibly be explained in terms of restrictions on export sales imposed
by group management. In contrast, the Swedish-owned tyre manufacturer, Gislaved, which has had no restrictions on exports, has been able
to manufacture in longer production runs. In the case of the other two
companies studied, the acquisition by foreign interests has not involved
any limitations. Thus, the expansion of the pump manufacturer, Flygt,
has been little influenced since the company was bought by ITT. In the
case of the cable manufacturer, IKO Kabel, also bought by ITT, it is
likely that development has been even more favourable than if the company had been acquired by one of the Swedish competitors who were
the potential alternatives to ITT.

The conclusion of this section is that companies which have direct
investments are responsible for a dominant proportion of Swedish exports and are also the companies which sell the greatest proportion of
their production as exports. However, as previously suggested, there
is a strong correlation between foreign investments, size of company
and the industry concerned and all three factors are clearly important
explanations of companies' export behaviour. Although multinationals
export more than other companies, we may none the less ask whether
foreign production means that exports from Sweden are, in fact, limited
— i.e. are less than they would have been otherwise. This is the most
controversial question in this context and we shall now attempt to answer
it.

How Does Increased Foreign Production Influence Exports?

Swedish industry's total foreign sales amounted to Skr 145 billion in
1978. Skr 89 billion of these were goods sold to foreign buyers, without
further contact with subsidiary sales companies or other intermediaries
(see Figure 9.1). Deliveries to foreign production companies amounted
to Skr 9 billion, of which roughly half consisted of materials and components used in production, whilst the remainder consisted of finished
goods. The sales value for the manufacturing subsidiaries abroad was

Skr 57 billion and Skr 4.5 billion of this total represented sales of goods manufactured by the parent company in Sweden. Only goods worth Skr 2 billion, out of the foreign manufacturing subsidiaries' total sales of Skr 57 billion, went to Sweden (see Figure 9.1). Therefore it is not possible to maintain that companies relocate their production to any great extent in order to sell goods back to Sweden. It is only in the clothing industry that exports to Sweden represent an appreciable proportion of sales by the foreign subsidiaries (see Table 9.4).

Table 9.3: Foreign Production by Subsidiaries in Relation to Total Swedish Foreign Sales (excl. Eastern bloc), 1965–78

Region	Production Abroad as Percentage of Total Foreign Sales			
	1965	1970	1974	1978
Developed Countries				
EEC	28	32	33	39
of which Original EEC	35	42	43	47
EFTA	13	14	12	16
(Nordic countries)	(10)	(12)	(12)	(14)
Other European	5	13	22	33
North America	47	37	38	46
Other developed countries	28	33	27	38
Developing Countries				
Africa, Asia	29	18	11	4
Latin America	42	49	46	65
All regions	27	29	28	34

Note: Total Foreign Sales = total Swedish exports + manufacturing subsidiaries sales − their imports from Swedish group companies.
Source: SOU (1982:27).

From 1965 to 1974, production in Sweden destined for exports increased at roughly the same pace as the expansion of capacity in the manufacturing facilities located abroad. In 1974 to 1978, however, foreign production began to increase considerably more rapidly than domestic production destined for export. As an indicator in this context, we may use the value of production in Swedish manufacturing subsidiaries abroad in relation to Swedish industry's foreign sales — this ratio increased from 28 per cent to 34 per cent in the period 1974–1978. The considerable shift in proportions is due more to poor development in the Swedish units in multinational groups, indicated in Chapter 1, than to any dynamic expansion in the foreign subsidiaries.

Figure 9.1: Swedish Industry's Sales Value and Foreign Sales, 1978

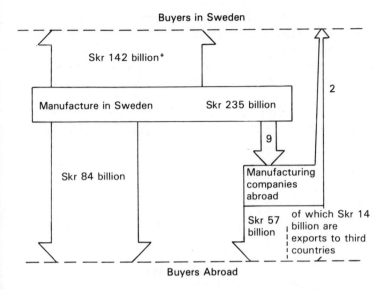

*Includes sales to Eastern bloc countries.

Source: Based on figures in SOU (1982:27).

The relative volume of foreign production varies considerably between regions. The highest figures occur in Latin America, where as much as 65 per cent of the total sales in 1978 consisted of locally manufactured products. The next highest proportion can be found in the original EEC countries, with figures approaching 50 per cent and, in third place, we find other industrialised or developed countries with around 40 per cent (see Table 9.3).

If we survey the entire period 1965–78, we find a clear shift towards increased local production and a reduced proportion of exports from Sweden. At the same time, however, we must remember that the proportion of Swedish exports destined for manufacturing subsidiaries has increased at about the same rate as foreign production. Referring to Figure 9.2, this means that flow A has increased in percentage terms as much as flow B but that flow B has increased considerably more than flow C.

However, it is not possible to draw any conclusions about the effects of foreign production on exports purely on the basis of these figures. We shall therefore proceed to discuss some relationships which are

Figure 9.2: Location of Manufacture of Foreign Sales of
Swedish Multinational Companies

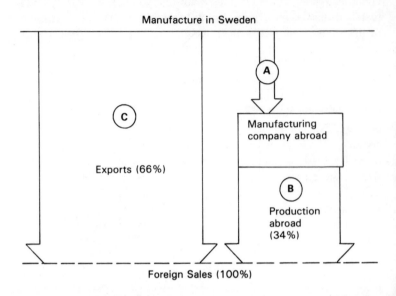

Note: A = Components and finished goods
      B = Manufacturing subsidiaries' sales (excl. their imports from Sweden)

normally used to indicate whether foreign production replaces exports.

The fact that certain manufacturing subsidiaries abroad sell part of
their production outside the host country has been presented as an argument supporting the case that foreign investments create negative export effects. It may, for example, be the case that a Swedish subsidiary
in West Germany replaces the Swedish parent company as an exporter
to Austria. Our information indicates that roughly a quarter of the sales
of manufacturing subsidiaries consisted of exports to third countries. As
we have previously mentioned, this proportion is lower than the export
intensity figures for foreign-owned companies in Sweden, but roughly
as high as the proportion indicated in a couple of studies of other countries. Even if the Swedish subsidiaries' export shares are not remarkably
high, they have none the less increased steadily since 1965, when the
proportion was only half as large as in 1978. Increased third-country
exports may be explained in terms of proximity to the market and the
fact that local production has become less important for the localisation
of foreign production. The higher proportion may also be partially due

to the fact that several multinational groups have begun to specialise their manufacturing processes amongst their existing subsidiaries in various countries, mainly due to increased advantages of scale, and to the fact that the countries concerned have different characteristics. An example of this often mentioned is that a country can have specifically advantageous terms for exports to a specific region.

Exports from Swedish production companies abroad show considerable variations from industry to industry (see Table 9.4). Two industries have a considerably higher export share than the average: the clothing industry (65 per cent) and the transport goods and vehicle industry (49 per cent). Vehicle industry exports are largely due to the output of two companies, in Belgium and the Netherlands, selling to other EEC countries. The clothing industry is, as already mentioned, the only industry with a high proportion of exports to Sweden. Apart from these special cases, almost the entire production of manufacturing subsidiaries outside Europe is sold in the host country. This may reflect the fact that these countries have local manufacturing requirements for sales in the country and that the establishment of manufacturing in these countries is largely the result of trade barriers.

Perhaps the most central question as regards the export effects of direct investments is whether exports decline rapidly to countries or regions where foreign production is increasing.

Table 9.5 indicates that there is an obviously negative correlation between the production growth of foreign subsidiaries and the increase in Swedish exports to various markets in the period 1965–78. In each of the four regions where the production growth of the foreign companies has been most marked — in the original EEC countries, in the rest of Europe and in Latin America — Swedish exports have expanded more slowly than in other regions. The remarkably strong percentage growth in foreign production in the rest of Europe (mainly Spain) should be viewed against a background of relative insignificance at the commencement of the period.

We have previously noted that the foreign production of Swedish industrial companies is increasing more than production in Sweden. An important question, therefore, is whether companies become more interested in localising production abroad when the proportion of foreign sales increases. If this is the case, it might mean that the continued internationalisation of industry will have negative export effects. The information presented in Table 9.6 indicates that it does not appear that companies with a high level of foreign sales have a larger proportion of their manufacturing abroad. The exception is the group of companies

Table 9.4: Sales and Foreign Trade, in Swedish Manufacturing Subsidiaries Abroad, by Industry, 1978 (Skr millions)

Industry	No. of subsidiaries	Skr millions				As percentage of sales		
		Sales	Exports	Exports to Sweden	Imports from Sweden	Exports	Exports to Sweden	Imports from Sweden
Food, beverages, tobacco	8	629	217	22	22	34	3	3
Textiles, clothing, leather, leather goods	24	442	288	172	56	65	39	13
Paper/pulp	21	2,848	640	6	190	22	4	9
Paper products, printing	50	3,178	635	139	294	20	4	9
Chemicals, rubber, plastics	79	4,166	425	135	520	10	3	12
Metal goods	123	8,094	864	105	2,297	11	1	28
Machinery	123	18,568	5,426	613	1,647	29	3	9
Electrical goods	78	8,129	565	220	1,226	7	3	15
Transport equipment	19	8,409	4,155	458	3,071	49	5	36
Other	43	2,525	485	79	64	10	3	2
Total	567	56,989	13,702	1,949	9,387	24	3	16

Source: SOU (1982:27).

Table 9.5: Growth in Subsidiaries' Foreign Production and in Swedish Exports to Various Regions, 1965–78

Region	Change (%)							
	Foreign Production				Swedish Exports			
	1965-70	1970-4	1974-8	1965-78	1965-70	1970-4	1974-8	1965-78
Industrialised Countries								
EEC	100	92	80	595	60	91	37	318
of which								
Original EEC	103	96	73	587	52	87	44	311
Other EEC	93	75	113	620	71	95	28	328
EFTA	90	80	68	464	87	100	26	370
(Nordic countries)	(120)	(94)	(56)	(570)	(79)	(93)	(35)	(365)
Other European	327	380	66	3,296	39	175	26	227
North America	16	94	116	384	76	83	56	404
Other developed countries	104	74	88	568	65	126	18	341
Developing Countries								
Africa, Asia	7	46	-30	13	98	154	126	1,037
Latin America	131	90	129	906	69	121	5	291
All regions	82	91	84	543	69	101	39	373

Source: SOU (1982:27).

with more than 80 per cent of their turnover abroad, where we find a higher proportion of foreign production than for the other groups.

A comparison between the degree of internationalisation for sales and production in the groups with foreign manufacturing in 1970 and 1978 (Table 3.6) indicates that the foreign shares have increased. Thus foreign sales represented more than 40 per cent of total group turnover in 67 groups in 1970 as compared with 82 groups in 1978. The share of foreign sales supplied by foreign manufacturing units has increased without correlation with the proportion of turnover represented by foreign sales. Thus the proportion has increased from 42 to 52 per cent for all corporate groups, which means that the Swedish multinational company group, on average, manufactured more than half its foreign sales abroad in 1978.

Table 9.6: Groups of Companies with Foreign Production in 1978, by proportion of total group turnover sold abroad in 1978

Foreign sales as percentage of total group turnover	No. of groups	Foreign sales (Skr million)	Average foreign sales (Skr million)	Foreign production as percentage of foreign sales
0–20	9	164	18	49
21–40	19	2,123	112	46
41–60	28	22,533	805	43
61–80	40	55,055	1,376	49
81–100	14	33,960	2,426	63
Total	110	113,835	1,035	52

Note: Foreign sales = Total group turnover less sales in Sweden by Swedish-based units. Production abroad = Foreign manufacturing subsidiaries' turnover less deliveries from Swedish-based units. Only groups of companies for which full information was available have been included.
Source: SOU (1982:27).

Thus, the overall picture which our studies have yielded is that foreign production has grown considerably more rapidly than export sales. In this section, we have attempted, in various ways, to illustrate correlations which might indicate that an increase in foreign production limits the growth of exports. On the other hand, econometric calculations undertaken point in another direction (SOU, 1982:27). By multiple regression analysis the impact from increased production abroad on exports from Sweden was judged to be insignificant. Somewhat inconclusive results point in the direction of a small positive effect. Two points suggest, in fact, that foreign production has not had any negative influence on exports. The first argument is that exports have developed least satisfactorily, relatively speaking, in markets which have high trade barriers. In other words it is not likely that there would have been any great increase in exports of finished products to these countries even if there had been no Swedish production companies located there. The second point is that foreign manufacturing gives rise to exports of components from Sweden which would not have occurred otherwise. The short-term export effect of direct investments, therefore, consists of changes in the exports of finished products and of components. If we wish to determine the direction of exports effects, it is necessary to examine the specific situations in some detail — as we have attempted in the case and industrial sector studies.

Exports of Finished Goods

The directives for our study were formulated thus: 'the Committee should study to what extent the establishment of foreign manufacturing facilities leads to a shift in exports of goods from Swedish to foreign production units'. We have *not* interpreted these directives to mean that our study should be exclusively confined to existing exports (i.e. if establishment abroad leads to a reduction of manufacturing in Sweden, which is compensated by new production abroad). The information we have gathered leads us to believe, in fact, that foreign investments are, generally speaking, expansive investments (i.e. that direct investments involve expansion of capacity rather than relocalisation of existing manufacturing).

In our following line of reasoning, we assume that potential alternative exports should be estimated, irrespective of whether the foreign investment represents relocation, expansion of capacity or is due to other reasons. As already discussed in Chapter 6, an attempt is normally made to estimate hypothetical exports by asking what would have happened if the company responsible for the investment had not invested abroad. Here we can imagine three possible alternatives:

(i)   The company could have undertaken investment in the home country instead, and then exported to the foreign market in question.
(ii) Another company would have undertaken the investment instead, in the host country.

(iii) The investment would not have taken place, either in the home country or in the host country.

In the first case, the direct investment can have a negative effect on the home country's balance of trade, since the company could have sold from its home base. In the second and third cases, foreign manufacturing would not have any significant effect on the home country's balance of trade since no exports would take place whatever the company decided. In our studies of companies and industries, the foreign investments investigated have been analysed with regard to whether the parent company, instead of manufacturing abroad, could have expanded production in the home country and sold exports to foreign markets. We can therefore roughly classify the investments studied in terms of the above three-way categorisation.

It has been difficult to find clear examples of investments of the type (i). Investments by Gambro in, for example, the United States come closest to investments of this type in the cases we have studied. Gambro manufactures hospital equipment and products for dialysis — the result of advanced research and development activities. Gambro's sales have increased rapidly and markedly over a short time span. Gambro achieved high export figures at an early stage, and has successively extended its foreign sales organisations by creating subsidiaries in around 15 countries. Some of the manufacturing operations have been progressively located abroad, to West Germany (1973), the USA (1974), Italy (1977) and Japan (1978). The American subsidiary is by far the largest, with a labour force which corresponds to 40 per cent of the number of employees in Sweden. Even before Gambro set up manufacturing facilities in the USA, the company had achieved a market share of around 20 per cent for disposable kidneys and in 1975 Gambro had a world market share of approximately 18 per cent for this product.

The reasons for establishment abroad given by the company were expressed in terms of costs and of the market. The cost aspects were customs duties and transport costs. However, we should observe that the company had considerable sales in the United States before the establishment of manufacturing facilities there, and it is probable that Gambro would have been able to continue to export a high proportion of the products that were later manufactured by the foreign subsidiary. The marketing reason for foreign establishment of manufacturing facilities was that foreign production led to better opportunities for contacts with the relevant institutions conducting research in the dialysis area in the countries concerned. This marketing aspect may, of course, be important for the future competitive strength of the company. If we confine ourselves to a short-term perspective, however, our judgement must necessarily be that the company would also have been able to achieve considerable foreign sales via exports, due to its advanced product line.

When we turn to the other foreign investments which have been studied we find that it is difficult to classify them unambiguously. Companies which have set up foreign manufacturing facilities have had what we have previously termed company-specific advantages in the form of differentiated products or advanced manufacturing techniques, but it is also the case that foreign establishment would not have taken place if there had not been special conditions in the host country. The most important factor, in this context, has been various forms of trade barriers. A trade barrier, for example a high tariff rate, functions here as comparative advantage for the host country, comparable with access to raw materials or a low level of wages. The higher the trade barrier, the more advantageous it becomes to pursue production in the country rather than exporting. In the telecommunications industry, for example, manufacturing operations are spread all over the world as a result of powerful preferences, in almost every country, in favour of locally manufactured equipment. Generally speaking, only minor markets are supplied via exports. The size of the market determines, to a large extent, whether there is a viable economic basis for local production. A study of Ericsson's establishment of manufacturing operations in Brazil, Colombia and Italy indicates that it would only have been feasible to export finished products to Colombia in any reasonable volume. We cannot, exclude the possibility that some other foreign company would have established manufacturing in Colombia if Ericsson had not acted first, and then Ericsson would have run the risk of losing the whole market if the authorities had later decided to tighten up their requirements and demand local production.

A factor that makes estimates of the effect on exports of finished goods more complex is that it is by no means certain that possible increased exports resulting from local manufacturing are formally credited to the manufacturing subsidiary. An example here is Ericsson's local production in Italy which is a necessary basis for exports from Sweden: it is the Ericsson group sales and installation subsidiary which is registered as the importer in Italy — not the manufacturing subsidiary in the same country.

Our studies have also indicated that many direct investments are not made with the intention of starting up manufacturing and sales of the companies' existing products or to exploit the host country's advantageous environment for industrial activities. When, for example, Atlas Copco purchased the American Jarva corporation, it was not because there was any intention to manufacture and sell Atlas Copco's products in the United States. The reason was, rather, that Atlas Copco wished to expand its product range within the group and strengthen the group's position. On the whole, this type of company purchase seems to have become increasingly common — especially in industries which we have chosen to characterise as global oligopolies. In such cases, direct investments may be seen as a step towards an expanded area of activity or as the strengthening of positions which have already been attained, thus hindering others from expanding. This type of company purchase over national frontiers results in effects corresponding to establishments of type (ii) above (i.e. they do not replace the export of finished products from the home country).

In order to describe, to some extent, what export effects may result from the increasingly common practice of international mergers between companies in the same industry, we shall briefly describe some details of Sandvik's purchase of the French company, Le Burin, and Electrolux's purchase of the American NUE corporation. Le Burin was a traditional and well-established manufacturer of rock drills. Its major customers were French mining companies and exports were minimal. Towards the end of the 1960s, Le Burin's management began to take the view that the company would find it difficult to compete in the technological development of the future. Since one of Le Burin's primary problems was difficulty in obtaining steel with consistent quality, it was natural to look for collaboration with a steel company. The result of Le Burin's search for a partner was its purchase by Sandvik — which already had a strong position on the French market — in 1971. Sandvik's main reason for purchasing Le Burin was to increase its market share and to reinforce its dominant position. If Sandvik had not purchased Le Burin, it is almost certain that some other competitor would have done so instead.

From Sandvik's point of view, the purchase meant that group turnover increased by Skr 20 million per year. 20 per cent of Le Burin's turnover consisted of products manufactured in Sweden which were sold under the Le Burin trade mark. The remaining 80 per cent of the turnover was manufactured from steel and cemented carbide imported from Sweden for assembly in France. If Sandvik had, instead, attempted to increase its market share by exporting drills from Sweden, aggressive competitive action would have been required. In view of the state-owned French mines' strong preferences in favour of French drills it is likely that the export alternative would only have resulted in a very small increase in sales.

Electrolux's purchase of the American vacuum cleaner manufacturer NUE, led to a dramatic increase in Electrolux's total vacuum cleaner production. Ultimately NUE represented 40 per cent of the group's manufacturing output, while Swedish output was only 10 per cent and the remaining manufacturing operations were spread over several countries. As a result of the purchase of NUE, Electrolux increased its market share in the United States from zero to 25 per cent. Electrolux's previous chances of exporting vacuum cleaners to the Unites States had not been particularly good. One reason was that the Electrolux trade mark was owned by an American company, the Electrolux Corporation. Another reason was that American vacuum cleaners differed in appearance from European products and, perhaps even more important, that Electrolux did not deem it feasible to export profitably from Sweden in view of the level of retail prices in the USA. Price is of great importance in this field, since vacuum cleaners are a standard product. Exports would only have been profitable for Electrolux if the retail price could have been raised, which might possibly have been achieved by choosing another form of distribution — for example, direct selling. The difficulties involved in familiarising consumers with a new trade mark and the costs of setting up a market organisation for direct selling were considered to be extremely high. The conclusion is, therefore, that it is hardly likely that any export sales to the United States would have taken place if Electrolux had not purchased NUE.

Sandvik and Electrolux's purchase of their foreign competitors, in common with the experience gained in other cases studied, indicates that direct investments in the form of the purchase of the foreign corporations do not limit Swedish exports of finished products. From the point of view of the Swedish economy, we might conclude that when foreign companies are for sale, a Swedish company, rather than any other company, might as well purchase them. Where foreign companies are purchased by Swedish enterprises, there may be opportunities for exports of components, etc., from Sweden, which we will discuss at a later stage.

Finally we turn to investments of type (iii), where foreign establishment can only be made by a specific company in a specific country. This type of investment is not typical of the outflow of Swedish direct investments and requires a combination of the company-specific and market-specific characteristics which permit the establishment of foreign facilities. The only example we have found in our studies of companies is the setting up of foreign operations by the furniture store chain, IKEA, for example, in West Germany and Switzerland. In view of IKEA's unique position, it is not likely that any other company would have established similar operations. IKEA is not an industrial company, however, since it does not manufacture any products itself. The same expansion of capacity by Swedish furniture manufacturers would probably not have taken place, if they had not been able to export to IKEA's furniture stores abroad. On the other hand, this is likely to be an oversimplification since we must also take into account such factors as IKEA's increased purchases from foreign suppliers as a result of its continuing internationalisation, and the fact that West Germany is now IKEA's largest market may mean that buying from Swedish furniture manufacturers will slowly decline in the future.

To summarise, we may say that the short-term effects of direct investments on exports of finished products appear to be varied. It is not possible to state that direct investments have predominantly negative or positive effects on exports. The best we can do is to speak of some kind of average effect. To determine the effect of a certain item of direct investment on exports of finished goods, we must assess the company's strength as an exporter, taking into account the nature of the product, the company's manufacturing technology and its marketing skill. We must also attempt to assess the advantages of pursuing local manufacturing in the country in question, taking into account, here, such factors as trade barriers of various kinds and also the competitive advantages of shifting production closer to the buyers. In assessing the long-term effects of exports, it is important to remember that the superiority necessary for achieving exports does not necessarily last for ever. It is rather a case of creating new advantages, in the case of Swedish companies, mainly involved in manufacturing and selling capital goods and other products which are sold to producers rather than consumers, consist of tying buyers closer to the Swedish manufacturer by means of a local presence. Thus, in many cases, local manufacturing is a necessary component in the marketing mix. It is therefore likely that local presence on various markets has often constituted the major advantage for Swedish exporters.

Exports of Components and Other Inputs Used in Manufacturing

Manufacturing subsidiaries abroad imported goods from Sweden worth approximately Skr 9 billion, corresponding to 16 per cent of their sales. This percentage has been largely unchanged since 1965. Roughly half the goods purchased by subsidiaries from Sweden consists of components and other input goods used in production. The other half is accounted for by finished products which are then sold without any further processing. Table 9.7 indicates that both the subsidiaries' import shares and the distribution amongst various product types vary considerably between the subsidiaries. Companies taken over by Swedish enterprises have a particularly low propensity to import from Swedish manufacturing units within the group. This is naturally due to the fact that these subsidiaries were previously independent foreign companies with well-developed supplier links. The purchase by Electrolux of NUE, which has previously been described, did not give rise to any appreciable exports of components, etc., from Sweden. The American company's output was four times as great as Electrolux's Swedish production and since the American company was both profitable and operational there were neither opportunities nor reasons for modifying the supplier structure. On the other hand, Sandvik's purchase of Le Burin did lead to the purchase of components, etc., from Sweden. This was both natural and expected, since Le Burin had previously experienced problems with its steel deliveries.

Table 9.7: Ratio of Imports by Companies with Foreign Subsidiaries, Established in Different Ways in the 1960s and 1970s

| | As percentage of sales | | | |
| | Imports | | Imports of components, etc. | |
	1970	1978	1970	1978
Subsidiaries established 1960–70				
Greenfield investments	24		19	
Ex-sales subsidiaries	36		5	
Acquisitions	8		5	
Subsidiaries established 1971–8				
Greenfield investments		21		14
Ex-sales subsidiaries		38		9
Acquisitions		10		6

Source: SOU (1982:27).

In the case of companies established through greenfield investments, there seems to be a relatively high propensity to import components for manufacturing and processing. Table 9.7 indicates that roughly two-thirds of those subsidiaries' imports from other companies within the group consisted of components, etc. Companies that had previously been sales companies show the highest import proportions, with imports averaging 36 to 38 per cent of their sales. However these imports largely consisted of goods which were to be resold.

Subsidiaries with manufacturing operations made total purchases from Sweden consisting of 49 per cent finished goods, 50 per cent components, etc. and 1 per cent of investment goods (see Table 9.8). When we estimate the positive effect on exports of components, etc., by foreign subsidiaries, we should be thinking in terms of a total of approximately Skr 4.5 billion. We can assume that exports of finished products, primarily to what were formerly sales companies, would have taken place in any case, even if no manufacturing activities had been undertaken.

Table 9.8: Imports into Foreign Subsidiaries from Swedish Parts of Swedish Multinational Groups, 1978

| Industry | Imports (Skr million) | Percentage of imports | | | |
		Finished goods	Components raw materials	Goods	Don't know*
Food, beverages and tobacco	22	95	5	0	0
Textiles, clothing, leather, leathergoods	56	43	52	5	4
Paper and pulp	190	3	97	0	0
Paper products, printing	294	50	50	0	0
Chemicals, rubber, plastics	520	46	50	4	1
Metal goods	2,297	75	25	0	13
Machinery	1,647	65	31	3	19
Electrical/electronics	1,226	61	38	1	12
Transport equipment	3,071	25	75	0	0
Other	64	45	53	2	13
Total	9,387	49	50	1	8

*The percentage distribution has been based on the data available. However, the Don't Know figures for the breakdown of imports into various categories have been significant in some cases, as indicated in the final column. If companies which have been unable to break down their imports differ appreciable from other companies, the values indicated in the Table will, of course, be misleading for some industries. There is, however, no *a priori* reason for believing this to be the case.
Source: SOU (1982:27).

The export of components initiated by foreign manufacturing companies is of minor significance seen in relation to Swedish industry's total foreign sales. Components, etc., corresponded to 8 per cent of the manufacturing subsidiaries' foreign sales and 3 per cent of Swedish industry's total foreign sales. If we make some simplifications, we could say that it would be a matter of indifference from the balance of payments point of view if it had been possible to achieve 8 per cent of the manufacturing subsidiaries' sales by exporting instead (if we can assume that the import proportion is the same for components as for finished products). On the other hand, it is probable that these components etc consist of high-technology items on which the product system which the company markets is centred. Thus, for example, the actual drill unit for Atlas Copco's drilling equipment is manufactured in Sweden, while the peripheral equipment is supplied locally in many cases. It is therefore likely that the value-added figure in such component exports is high.

We have not been able to obtain a clear picture of how exports of components, etc., to manufacturing subsidiaries have changed over time. In total, as has already been mentioned, we can say that the proportion of imports from Sweden to the foreign manufacturing subsidiaries has been virtually unchanged since 1965. This could be interpreted as an indication that the foreign subsidiaries maintain their level of imports from Sweden and do not take over further stages in production or do not make increasing use of local subcontractors and suppliers. An alternative interpretation is that new subsidiaries import a high proportion of their requirements from Sweden but that this proportion gradually drops. The arrival of new subsidiaries on the scene over the period studied could explain why the average proportion has not, in fact, declined. Specific details obtained in our studies of companies tend to support this interpretation. Figure 9.3 shows how Atlas Copco's manufacturing subsidiaries abroad have increased their turnover and imports from Sweden. In 1965 the manufacturing subsidiaries' imports from Sweden represented almost 45 per cent of turnover, but by 1978 the proportion had dropped to below 18 per cent.

Information supplied by Volvo can serve to illustrate how internationalisation and other factors influence the company's purchasing and subcontractor systems. Today, Volvo has more that 1,600 suppliers and purchases more than 200,000 different components and items from more than 30 countries. Special purchasing offices in, for example, Belgium, Japan, the Netherlands and the United States administer the purchasing operations. As already mentioned in Chapter 3, the proportion of items

Figure 9.3: Atlas Copco Group — Foreign Sales and Exports from Sweden to Foreign Subsidiaries in 1965 and 1978 (Skr million)

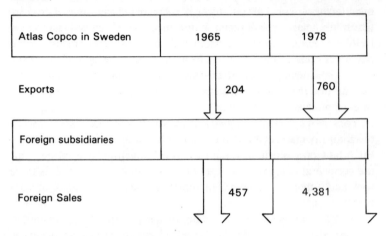

Source: SOU (1982:15).

bought in Sweden has steadily fallen from 55 per cent to 30 per cent over the period 1967–83.

One explanation for the decline in the proportion of deliveries of materials and components from Sweden is that these items have become more technologically complex. Products such as pumps and electronic components are only produced by companies in the major automobile-manufacturing countries. Despite several attempts, Volvo has not been successful in initiating any domestic manufacture of such components. At the moment, for example, Volvo typically purchases plastic and press-ed steel items for the interiors of its cars in Sweden. We cannot exclude the possibility that technological development will lead to a further increase in the complexity of components and that the proportion of purchases abroad, as a result, will also increase.

To some extent, the increased proportion of purchases abroad is linked with the increased internationalisation of production. Thus, the acquisition of the Dutch car manufacturer, DAF, meant that the proportion of purchases abroad by the Volvo group increased, since the Dutch plant had a different supplier structure. In the case of Volvo's investments in plants in such countries as Malaysia, Canada and Peru, the authorities have required that certain purchases must be placed locally. Indeed, the Canadian authorities have required that Volvo's factory in Canada should sell certain products to group companies in other countries. Volvo's production in its plants in Belgium has now attained volumes where it has become profitable to utilise local suppliers of certain components to a greater extent. Local purchases in Belgium primarily involve products which are heavy or bulky and therefore involve high transport costs. Deliveries from Sweden of items such as batteries, seat covers and other passenger compartment items have therefore been replaced by local purchases. In order to be able to place orders for even larger volumes, the Belgian subsidiary now purchases some parts which are then sent to the Swedish plants.

Thus we can see a number of explanations for the internationalisation of Volvo's purchasing function. Increased technological complexity has led to concentration and specialisation in industries supplying components and parts. Furthermore it has become increasingly profitable to utilise local subcontractors when foreign production rises in volume. In some countries, the authorities require that local subcontractors must be used if manufacturing and sales are to be permitted. Finally, Volvo prefers to deal with several suppliers of the same components to avoid excessive dependence on any individual subcontractor. This preference contributes to, and necessitates, increased international purchasing.

To summarise, we may note that Swedish-owned manufacturing subsidiaries abroad purchase a proportion of their components, etc., from Sweden. If there had been no manufacturing abroad, exports of components would not have taken place either. The positive effects on Swedish exports which foreign manufacturing gives rise to are, however, extremely limited in comparison with Swedish industry's foreign sales as a whole. Information gathered from the companies studied also seems to indicate that an increasing degree of internationalisation seems to lead to a more international purchasing pattern. This change is, however, largely caused by the concentration and specialisation of the supplying industries resulting from the technological development process. In our view, the positive effect that establishment of foreign manufacturing facilities has on Swedish component exports is minor. In the long term, it is not at all certain that it is a positive effect, since advanced internationalisation of manufacture can also mean that the Swedish groups' plants in Sweden are increasingly supplied by foreign subcontractors.

Summary

Firstly the study shows that multinationals increased their exports more than the rest of Swedish industry. Companies with foreign manufacturing facilities increased their share of total Swedish exports from 40 to 46 per cent in the period 1965–78. In the same period, the multinationals' share of total employment in industry rose from 32 to 37 per cent. If we also include companies which set up foreign manufacturing in the period studied, the multinationals' share of Swedish exports was 58 per cent. Multinationals also demonstrated the highest export intensity (i.e. exports in relation to the value of production).

Foreign-owned companies in Sweden had a higher export intensity than national companies or Swedish subsidiaries abroad. Foreign-owned corporations sold more that half their exports to other companies within the same group. A second point is that production in Sweden destined for export increased at roughly the same pace as the expansion of capacity in the foreign manufacturing subsidiaries over the period 1965–74. In the period 1974–8, however, foreign production began to increase considerably more rapidly than domestic production destined for export. Exports of components and other products destined for manufacturing subsidiaries have, however, increased at roughly the same rate as foreign production. These exports comprised only a relatively small proportion of the multinationals' total exports.

Details of the sales of foreign subsidiaries do not support the thesis that companies have shifted their production out of Sweden to any great extent so as to sell their goods back to Sweden. Only Skr 2 billion of the foreign companies' total sales of Skr 57 billion went to Sweden. Subsidiaries' total sales outside the host country comprised roughly a quarter of turnover. This proportion was only half as large in 1965.

There is a clear negative correlation between the growth of production of foreign companies and the growth of Swedish exports in various markets. Exports to markets with high trade barriers increased least. It is therefore not at all certain that there would have been any appreciably higher sales in these countries if there had not been any Swedish production companies there.

Production by Swedish multinationals has been markedly internationalised. Thus, the proportion of foreign sales which are manufactured abroad has increased from 42 per cent in 1970 to 52 per cent in 1978. This increase is a general one and not correlated with foreign sales' share of total turnover and it does not seem that companies with a high proportion of foreign sales also have a high proportion of foreign production.

The exception is the group of companies with more than 80 per cent of their turnover abroad where the proportion of foreign sales was 63 per cent in 1978. Since both foreign sales and foreign production increased more than domestic sales and domestic production, we would be justified in speaking of a shift of emphasis, away from Sweden, in the Swedish multinational companies.

In our interpretation of the empirical results, we feel that it is impossible to classify the short-term export effects as broadly positive or negative. Some foreign investments have had an immediate positive effect on exports from Sweden, while others have resulted in a slower increase in exports, in the period immediately after the establishment of foreign facilities, than would otherwise have been the case. A third category of investments, primarily certain acquisitions of companies, may not have influenced exports either in a positive or negative direction. The interesting question is what long-term effects direct investments have had on exports. As we have previously indicated in connection with our discussion of technological development and competitiveness, we consider that the establishment of foreign manufacturing facilities has been one way for the major Swedish companies to maintain their position within various international oligopolies. If Swedish companies had refrained from making use of this strategy, most of them would probably not have attained their current positions in their industries and many of them would probably have been taken over by foreign competitors or been forced to move into new fields of activity with less emphasis on technology. The consequences of such developments, at a given exchange rate, would have been lower exports. With a given cost structure, direct investments have thus had positive long-term consequences for exports, since they have contributed to strengthening the competitive situation of Swedish-based units within the Swedish multinationals. This is not to say that it would not have been possible in some cases to achieve greater exports by marginally reducing direct investments. In most cases, however, it is extremely difficult to predict with any reliability the future export effects of individual direct investments.

10 EMPLOYMENT

In the American studies from the early 1970s which have already been referred to in Chapter 6, it was assumed that the effects of an outflow of direct investments on exports and on employment were analogous. It was argued that if exports increased, greater production in the home country can be assumed, which in turn, requires more personnel. Thus it should be possible to calculate the increase in employment on the basis of the figures for export increases. However, as indicated earlier, the correlation between the Swedish industry's production volume and the number of employees has become progressively weaker in the post-war period. Increased exports do not necessarily result in a corresponding increase in employment in industry. It would therefore be more correct to say that increased production resulting from any possible positive export effects tends to counteract a reduction in employment, rather than creating an increase in employment.

We have also made the assumption that direct investments have analogous effects on exports and employment. We do not, therefore, examine any employment effects in the cases and industries studied, in this chapter, but refer the reader to the discussion in Chapter 9 covering export effects. The aim now is to look instead at the total number of employees in multinational and other companies, examining changes in the various companies' share of total employment. We have not, however, considered it possible to estimate the change in the total number of employees which has resulted from direct investments.

In the discussion of American studies of the outflow of direct investments it was maintained that a slight net effect on total employment may have somewhat complex implications. The jobs that are created and the jobs which disappear as a result of foreign manufacturing by companies are in fact not of the same type. The new jobs generally have a different character and require different training. Personnel who are made redundant or who are not employed as a result of an expansion of manufacturing abroad are not automatically eligible for the new jobs created. In a long-term analysis, the effects on the distribution of different types of jobs may be just as important as effects on total industrial employment. Using data extracted from statistics produced jointly by the unions and the Swedish Employers Federation, it has proved possible to analyse the breakdown of

136

employee functions and levels of competence and skill for various categories of company.

The Development of Employment for Various Categories of Company

We will illustrate the effects of direct investments on employment in industry in Sweden, using figures for the total number of employees for various company categories in Sweden and for Swedish subsidiaries abroad. A typical problem which arises when studying changes in employment over time is that the companies comprising the population to be studied also change. Some companies disappear, new companies are created and certain companies become multinational in the period studied. In order to give a reasonably fair picture of changes in employment in companies with, and without, direct investments, we have only included those companies which have belonged to the same category throughout the relevant period (see Figure 10.1). However, this inevitably means that companies which have disappeared between 1966 and 1979 are not included. The population used thus represents a positive selection to some extent, especially for the national companies category.

The shape of the curves in Figure 10.1 reflects the fact that employment in industry in Sweden peaked in the mid-1960s and then slowly declined. Since Figure 10.1 only includes companies which have survived throughout the full period, the curves give us a more positive picture of total employment change than if all companies had been included. The multinationals which have continued operations throughout the period have, broadly speaking, unchanged employment figures from 1966 to 1979. Swedish national companies show a larger percentage increase, although the employment opportunities they represent are not so large in terms of absolute numbers.

Foreign-owned companies show the largest percentage increase but account for only a small proportion of the total number of employees in Sweden. In 1978, approximately 6 per cent of employees in industry worked for companies at least 50 per cent owned by foreign corporations. The relatively large increase in the number of employees in foreign-owned companies is not necessarily a result of an increase in production in Sweden. In fact, foreign-owned companies have a high and increasing proportion of purely sales functions in their activities — corresponding to 24 per cent of turnover in 1977. Many foreign-owned industrial companies in Sweden, in common with Swedish-owned manufacturing

Figure 10.1: Employment for Various Company Categories
for 1966–72, 1973–7 and 1977–9 (companies remaining in
the same category through the period) (thousands)

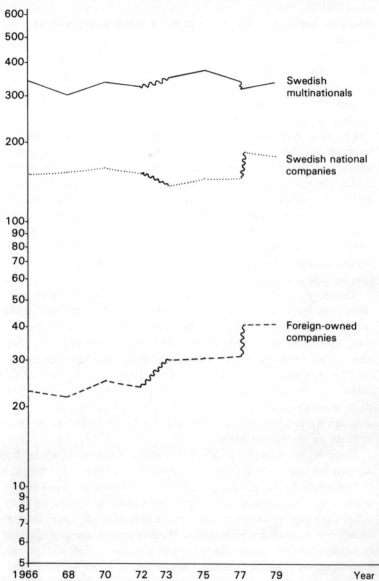

Source: SOU (1982:15).

companies abroad. also have the character of sales subsidiaries with manufacturing activities added. Increased employment in the foreign-owned companies can therefore be explained to some extent by expansion of purely sales activities. Our conclusion is that it is not possible to note any appreciable differences between the development of employment in multinational companies and other companies, if we confine ourselves to a study of companies remaining in the same category throughout the period. If, however, we compare the number of employees in all multinationals and all national companies at various points in time, the picture will be rather different.

Table 10.1: Number of Employees in Swedish Industry, in Swedish Groups with Foreign Investments and in Foreign Manufacturing Subsidiaries, in total and for the 20 largest foreign investors, 1965–78

	1965	1970	1974	1978
Swedish industry	938,915	921,780	929,200	874,230
Swedish companies with foreign investments	325,880	395,990	431,740	416,235
as percentage of Swedish industry	35	43	46	48
Foreign manufacturing subsidiaries	147,805	182,650	219,625	227,825
as percentage of Swedish industry	16	20	24	26
20 largest Swedish multinationals	219,490	247,160	271,530	259,530
as percentage of Swedish industry	23	27	29	30
Swedish foreign subsidiaries	133,450	158,390	189,520	196,900
as percentage of Swedish industry	14	17	20	23

Source: SOU (1982:27);

Table 10.1 indicates that the total number of employees working for all Swedish multinational companies increased by almost 100,000 between 1965 and 1978. This increase includes employees acquired as the result of mergers and acquisitions. Employment in the Swedish units within Swedish multinationals increased until 1974, and then declined. Since the number of employees in other companies declined even more, the proportion of employees in Swedish multinational companies increased in the 1970s to 48 per cent in 1978.

The previously noted rapid growth of Swedish multinationals' foreign production, is reflected in the figures for the number of employees working for foreign production companies. The proportion of foreign employees in relation to the number of employees in Swedish industry increased from 16 per cent to 26 per cent in 1978. We also find in Table 10.1 that 86 per cent of the employees in Swedish manufacturing subsidiaries abroad work for one of the 20 largest companies.

Figure 10.2 shows how changes in employment in the Swedish units of companies investing abroad can be broken down into components for the four-year period 1974–8: the number of employees in the Swedish units declined by 33,000 or 8 per cent. 21,000 of the total for employees in 1978 worked for companies acquired within the previous four years. These 21,000 individuals were not an addition to total industrial employment in Sweden, but rather represented a shift between various groups of companies, on the assumption that companies which were taken over would have been able to survive even if the take-overs had not occurred.

Figure 10.2: Changes in Employment in Swedish Units of Swedish Multinational Groups (remaining in the category), from 1974 to 1978

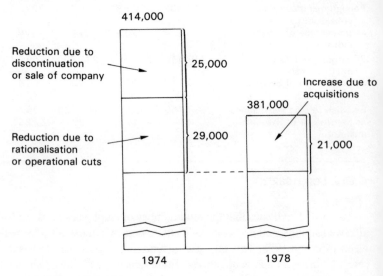

Source: SOU (1982:27);

The trend indicated by Figure 10.2 for the total group of companies with foreign investments can also be traced in the industry studies. In the case of large international companies such as Atlas Copco, Fläkt and Sandvik, group employment has increased in the foreign units, while the number of employees in Sweden has been relatively unchanged in the 1970s. The increase in employment abroad can be largely explained, as we shall see, by the acquisition of foreign companies and their coordination into the group.

Figure 10.3 links the increase in the number of employees in manufacturing subsidiaries abroad to the form of expansion — whether other companies have been purchased or subsidiaries set up. Some increase of personnel in the existing companies occurred in the period 1960–70. In the 1970s, however, employment in existing companies fell and the growth in employment shown for foreign subsidiaries is largely explained by the purchase of other companies. An important explanation of the decline reported for existing companies is, however, that several subsidiaries previously owned by Swedish companies have been transferred to foreign interests in the period studied.

Figure 10.3: Number of Employees in Swedish Manufacturing Subsidiaries Abroad, 1960–70 and 1970–8

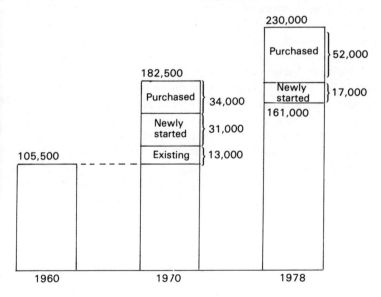

Source: SOU (1982:27).

Structure of Employment for Various Company Categories

Within the total framework of reductions in industrial employment, there have been changes in the proportions of workers and permanent staff. Similar changes within these two categories can also be seen as regards, for example, job descriptions and the degree of competence or skill required. One of the studies (SOU, 1983:16) has made use of labour market statistics to analyse the effects of direct investments on the employment structure.

In Swedish industry, there has been a shift in the employment structure from workers to staff (see Table 10.2). The proportion of staff employees increased from 26 per cent to 29 per cent from 1966 to 1978. Multinational companies have a higher proportion of staff than national companies — 34 per cent for multinationals compared with 27 per cent for national companies in 1978. This difference increased between 1966 and 1974, while the increase is the same in percentage terms, for multinational companies and for total Swedish industry between 1974 and 1978. Foreign-owned companies have a considerably higher proportion of staff (45 per cent in 1974) than other companies. This may be linked with the fact that foreign-owned companies have a higher proportion than other corporate categories of purely sales functions.

The greater importance of purely sales activities in foreign-owned companies and the fact that they are 'less industrial' than other company categories may well explain why foreign-owned companies have the highest proportion of staff active in the marketing field. The data also indicates that the proportion of staff working in the marketing function is the same in national and multinational companies. In addition, the two categories have roughly the same proportion of staff involved in control functions. The real distinction between multinational and purely national companies lies in the proportion of staff employees working in the technical development function. The multinationals' high proportion is largely due to the characteristics of the ten largest groups. Most of these companies are in the engineering industry, which has a heavy emphasis on technological development but a low proportion of employment in the marketing function. Although the employment structure can be partly explained in terms of the type of industry involved, it is also true that multinational companies have higher proportions working in technological development than their national equivalents in the engineering industry and associated sectors.

The figures for the total number of staff employees and their distribution over the various functions between 1965 and 1978 indicate

Table 10.2: Workers and Staff Employed by Various Company Categories, 1966–78

	1966			1970			1974			1978		
	Workers	Staff	Staff (%)	Workers	Staff	Staff (%)	Workers	Staff	Staff (%)	Workers	Staff	Staff (%)
Total industry	685,574	328,358	26	674,921	246,657	27	678,631	250,571	27	618,734	255,496	29
National companies	179,646	62,407	26	144,449	51,699	26	145,005	55,604	28			
Multinationals	177,249	78,850	31	207,843	103,299	33	231,842	118,799	34	230,612	129,407	36
Foreign companies	22,987	15,187	40	31,719	24,329	43	37,999	31,496	45			
Total Sample	379,882	156,444	29	384,011	179,327	32	414,846	205,899	33	237,819	132,551	36
As Percentage of total industry												
National companies	26	26		21	21		21	22				
Multinationals	26	33		31	42		34	47		37	51	
Foreign companies	3	6		5	10		6	13				
Total	55	66		57	73		61	82		38	52	

Source: SOU (1983:16).

that there are clear differences between the ten largest multinational companies and the next group in terms of size (the eleventh to twentieth largest). The top ten multinationals show the greatest increase in the number of staff and the greatest percentage increase within the various company functions for the whole of the period under study. This might well indicate that the largest Swedish multinationals are increasingly acquiring the character of administrative and development units on Swedish soil, while the production function is being progressively localised abroad. In the case of the smaller multinationals, it is possible that manufacturing companies abroad are more integrated in the functional structure.

As regards changes in the worker category, we have attempted to indicate to what extent the multinationals have control systems and production technologies which differ from other companies and which lead to a different worker structure. Information about worker structures in companies remaining in the same category throughout 1974 to 1980 (Table 10.3) indicates that national companies have the highest proportion of skilled workers. The multinationals had the highest proportion of intermediary categories as regards skills. This may reflect the fact that multinationals have large plants, frequently characterised by mass production methods. Foreign-owned companies have the largest proportion of unskilled workers, which may be due to the fact that production operations in these companies may consist largely of assembly, which demands fewer skills. However, these distinctions between ownership categories are closely tied to the industry involved. If a comparison is made between the three company categories on an industry basis, we find deviations from the overall pattern. It is also interesting to note that the ten largest multinationals have the lowest proportion of skilled workers — probably due to mass production methods, as explained above. Other multinationals have roughly the same proportion of skilled workers as their national equivalents.

Changes between 1974 and 1980 (see Table 10.3) indicate a shift in the case of multinational companies from the unskilled group to the semi-skilled group, reflecting a rise in the average level of skills demanded. A roughly similar shift has occurred in the foreign-owned group — although we still find a higher proportion of unskilled workers here. The national category of companies — with the most even distribution amongst skills requirements — show a slight shift from the semi-skilled group to the unskilled group.

The total reduction in the number of employees in industry has thus taken place in parallel with changes in the composition of the labour

Table 10.3: Labour-Force Structure in Companies Remaining in the Same Category (%).

	National		Multinational		Foreign		All Companies	
	1974	1980	1974	1980	1974	1980	1974	1980
Skilled	36	35	22	23	22	24	23	24
semi-skilled	38	35	56	61	41	46	53	57
unskilled	26	29	22	16	37	30	24	19
Total	100	100	100	100	100	100	100	100
Number of employees	14,495	14,182	117,979	100,327	11,354	9,872	143,828	124,381
Number of companies	90		114		38		242	

force. The proportion of staff employees has increased. The reduced proportion of workers has also involved a shift in favour of jobs which require a more highly skilled labour force. These changes have been most marked in the multinational category but we should note that changes in the multinationals between 1978 and 1980 have been in the reverse direction.

These changes are consistent with changes in the fields of technological development, competitiveness and exports described in previous chapters. Industry based in Sweden has experienced structural change, moving towards products and manufacturing processes characterised by a greater degree of technological complexity. It is difficult to isolate and distinguish the total effects of direct investments on developments on employment, since so many other factors are involved. The fact that the number of employees has declined, even in companies which seem to have strengthened their competitive situation by means of foreign direct investments, can be explained, to some extent at least, by technological development which made an improvement in the competitive position possible and by a system of incentives which encouraged the rationalisation of production processes.

Summary

Against a background of a slow decline in industrial employment since 1965, multinational companies have increased their share of employment from 35 to 48 per cent. The greater part of this increase can be explained, however, in terms of the increasing number of companies that have become multinational and that new companies have been integrated into multinational groups. In the latest period studied — 1974–8 — the acquisition of companies has not compensated for the reduction in the number of employees resulting from rationalisation and the shutting down of older plants. If we exclude the acquisition of companies, the multinationals' Swedish operations have experienced roughly the same development pattern as other company categories.

The case studies of the development of employment in the foreign-owned companies do not show any clear trends. Variations can be attributed to the roles allocated to foreign-owned subsidiaries by the strategy of the company group. In total, the foreign-owned companies were responsible for the largest percentage increase in employment. This increase was, however, relatively insignificant in absolute terms, and not at all comparable with increased employment in Swedish multinationals abroad.

230,000 employees worked for Swedish manufacturing subsidiaries abroad in 1978, a figure which corresponds to 26 per cent of employment in Swedish industry. The corresponding figure for 1965 was 16 per cent. Despite these figures, it does not seem likely that the expansion of foreign manufacturing has restricted an increase in employment in the Swedish units of Swedish multinationals. The figures indicate that employment in existing foreign subsidiaries is declining, while additions to the total number of employees abroad can be explained by the purchase or setting-up of new companies. Our analysis indicates that these investments did not normally replace comparable investments in Sweden, but this does not necessarily mean that there are no short-term negative effects in some cases. If the level of costs is taken as given, direct investments mean that the level of employment is higher than it would have otherwise been, due to improved competitiveness and higher exports. This implies a structural change in employment with a shift towards higher levels of skill and competence. We find, in fact, that the proportion of staff employees has increased and that the level of skills required of workers has also risen.

11 INDUSTRIAL STRUCTURE

The term 'industrial structure' is normally used as a collective description of various characteristics for a particular country's total industry. Important examples of such characteristics are the relative significance of industries such as engineering and chemicals, the degree of company concentration (i.e. their number and size) within the various industries, the technology of companies and their regional localisation. The total picture of industry in terms of the various dimensions which jointly comprise its structure is the result of a long historical process in which foreign direct investments have been one influential factor. Thus, structural effects can be said to be more comprehensive than foreign direct investments, on the one hand, but they are also more difficult to envisage, on the other hand.

There are several reasons for taking a close look at the picture of industry in a country and at changes in its industrial structure. For instance, it is possible to form an opinion of how efficient industry is, from social and economic perspectives, by studying industrial structure. A social and economic assessment can be based on industrial organisation theory which assumes correlations between concentration of companies, product differentiation and economies of scale, on the one hand, and industry's behaviour as regards pricing and other competitive measures. Various patterns of behaviour can then be seen as advantageous or problematical from the point of view of society and the total economy. Thus, this perspective allows us to use industrial structure to indicate positive or negative features of the economy and the central question in this context is whether efficiency gains resulting from increased company concentration and large-scale operations outweigh possible losses resulting from monopoly.

Another reason for taking a close look at industrial structure is that it has decisive effects on a country's international competitiveness and thus on its economic standard of living. The relative significance of various industries within the economy gives us an opportunity to form an opinion as to whether the country's production effort involves goods which face satisfactory levels of demand, both domestically and abroad, and both currently and in the immediate future. Table 11.1 gives a very broad classification of various industries in Sweden, indicating their share of world markets and the status of international demand. A classification

147

of this type gives a rough picture of Sweden's current and anticipated competitive strength, assuming that the country can and wishes to compete in the expansive commodity areas. Clothing has been one of the most rapidly expanding commodity groups in international trade in the 1970s. However, Swedish industry would probably not have been more competitive if a higher proportion of Swedish exports had consisted of clothing products in the early 1970s (SIND, 1981:3. p. 33).

Table 11.1: Products of Various Industries, Classified as High/Low in Terms of World-Trade Growth and Major/Minor in Importance for Swedish Exports

Swedish share of world market in 1971	World-trade growth 1971–9, at current prices	
	Low	High
Major	Mining Paper/pulp Iron/steel Machinery Shipbuilding	Wood products Metal goods Electrical/electronics
Low	Food Textiles Printing Non-ferrous metals	Clothing Chemicals Oil refineries Plastics Non-metalliferous mining Transport equipment Instruments

The non-economic effects represent a third aspect of industrial structure. The more one-sided a country's dependence on certain industries is, the more we find that the country is dependent on imported products. A concentrated structure, with a few large companies, can also be a sign of reduced flexibility and of difficulty in adjusting quickly than a structure characterised by many smaller companies. From the social point of view, small companies or places of work that are not inhumanly large may be considered preferable. A good geographical spread will also be found compatible with the ambition to differentiate industry in various regions of the country in question.

Although the effects of foreign investments on industrial structure are of interest for a number of reasons, very few studies have looked at this question. In a major American study of the effects of direct investments (Bergsten *et al.*, 1978, p. 213) it was noted that 'the impact of US investments abroad on the structure and performance of US domestic industry has been largely ignored, perhaps because the issue is subtle and complex'. This study considered the question of whether foreign investments by multinationals influenced their corporate profitability and competitive status *vis-à-vis* other American companies on the domestic market. Foreign investments were here assumed likely to be advantageous for home market activities for a number of reasons. The first point is that foreign investments can be seen as backward integration in the direction of raw materials and as forwards integration into new markets, thus giving multinational companies advantages over companies which only imported or exported. Furthermore, overseas activities give companies a broader base for the allocation of fixed costs and a better spread of risks than a purely domestic company can achieve. Finally, international activities may also lead to a more favourable taxation position. Using statistical analysis, the study found that there was a clear correlation between the volume of foreign investments and profitability on the home market. This correlation also applied within the same industry, even if size differences between multinationals and other companies were taken into account (Bergsten *et al.*, 1978, p. 245).

We have chosen to tackle the effects of direct investments on industrial investments in two sections. In the first section we discuss how direct investments may explain the distribution of industrial companies over various industries. The second section takes up the question of how international investments affect competition, concentration and technology in various industries.

Effects of Direct Investments on the Status of Various Industries

We can explain the possible effects of direct investments on the relative strength of various industries in two ways. Firstly, it may be the case that multinationals, exploiting their superiority, contribute to a redirection of consumption over to products manufactured by such large companies. The result will then be that the industrial production increases more in some industries than in others.

Direct investment theory, which states that it is a precondition for foreign production that the company investing abroad has some company-specific competitive advantage, gives us another possible explanation. Company-specific advantages occur mainly where products are differentiated (i.e. when they are not identical with other companies' products). Product distinctions can be based on a technological situation involving complicated manufacturing processes or a product which is given unique, or at least unusual, characteristics. The product may be also marketed in a way that emphasises its differentiation (for example, through the use of trade marks or company-owned sales channels). We are therefore most likely to find multinational companies in industries or sub-industries where there are opportunities for selling differentiated products. It is also the case that demand in a society with rising standards of living increasingly shifts towards differentiated products.

Our results confirm that the most rapid growth has taken place in industries characterised by differentiated products. From the Swedish point of view, the engineering industry is an important and prominent example in this context (see Tables 11.2 and 11.3). As a measure of the products' degree of differentiation, we have used research and development intensity and the number of technical staff employed. It is also worth noting that Swedish-controlled activities abroad have been dominated by the engineering industry.

Table 11.3 shows that companies which are active at an international level are responsible for the major share of the engineering industry's added value. In the iron, steel and non-ferrous metal industries we see, in contrast, a dramatic reduction in the value-added share. This reduction can be explained in terms of reverses suffered by Swedish multinational companies. The various changes in industrial structure can be summarised in a nutshell if we say that internationally active companies are responsible for increases in the expanding industries and for the reductions in declining industries. These changes might be an indication that internationally active companies have greatly influenced the structural change which has already taken place. Taking a total view, internationally active companies represent an increasing proportion of Swedish industry. Thus, the value-added proportion achieved by the national companies in the areas selected has fallen from 37 per cent in 1966 to 31 per cent in 1977.

We thus find it established that there is a correlation between foreign investments and the relative importance of various industries in Sweden. The next question to examine, then, is how direct investments influence differences in industry structure between various countries. An

Table 11.2: Structural Descriptive Variables for Various Industries

ISIC		Capital intensity[1]	Technical personnel intensity[2]	Human capital intensity[3]	R&D intensity[4]	% of Industry			
						Value added		Exports	
						1963	1978	1963	1978
2	Mines	484	83	109	16	3.4	2.1	5.2	3.0
31	Food, Beverages, Tobacco	59	42	93	36	12.7	9.9	3.2	1.8
32	Textiles	27	29	81	14	7.0	3.5	2.2	2.9
33	Wood Products	91	31	90	7	7.6	8.5	8.1	6.5
341	Paper/Pulp	455	62	104	30	10.0	10.8	25.1	19.1
342	Printing	18	28	118	2	9.0	7.1	0.3	0.5
351, 352	Chemical Industry	118	173	109	189	} 6.0	} 9.3	} 5.5	} 9.3
353, 354	Oil/Coal Products	296	246	116	130				
355, 356	Rubber/Plastics	80	64	92	36				
361, 362	China, Earthware, Glass	39	50	89	32				
369	Bricks, Cement, Other Mineral Products	134	78	99	68	3.9	3.0	1.0	1.0
37	Ferrous, Non-Ferrous Metals	219	101	106	51	5.7	5.5	8.1	10.2
381	Metal Products	45	65	95	45	} 25.7	} 30.1	} 26.2	} 33.1
382	Machinery	48	143	102	148				
384	Transport Equipment (excl. Shipbuilding)	34	163	102	307				
383	Electrical/Electronics	24	204	104	277	6.1	7.7	5.0	7.2
3841	Shipbuilding	57	103	105	—	2.7	2.2	9.9	4.8
39	Other Manufacturing	27	78	87	177	0.4	0.6	0.4	0.6
2, 3	Total Industry	100	100	100	100	100.0	100.0	100.0	100.0

1. Installed KW per employee in 1978.
2. Technical personnel as percentage of total employees in 1975.
3. Wages and salaries per employee 1978.
4. R&D as percentage of value-added.
Source: SCB (1977:23).

Table 11.3: Value Added for Various Company Categories in 1966, 1972 and 1977, in absolute figures (Skr million) and as percentage share of each industry, and sample's share of total value added to Swedish industry

Industry	Company category	1966		1972		1977	
		Skr million	%	Skr million	%	Skr million	%
ISIC 31	Swedish multinational	266	19	398	10	639	10
	Foreign-owned	87	6	213	5	731	11
	Swedish national	1,022	74	3,485	85	5,132	79
	Total for industry	1,375	7	4,096	12	6,502	11
ISIC 32	Swedish multinational	254	31	486	44	593	39
	Foreign-owned	10	1	113	10	159	10
	Swedish national	550	68	503	46	772	51
	Total for industry	814	4	1,102	3	1,524	2
ISIC 33	Swedish multinational	227	40	282	23	747	32
	Foreign-owned	9	2	13	1	20	1
	Swedish national	337	59	915	76	1,590	67
	Total for industry	573	3	1,210	3	2,357	4
ISIC 34	Swedish multinational	1,112	33	3,023	56	5,875	61
	Foreign-owned	126	4	155	3	187	2
	Swedish national	2,151	63	2,234	41	3,533	37
	Total for industry	3,389	17	5,412	15	9,595	15
ISIC 35	Swedish multinational	513	42	1,233	54	2,211	48
	Foreign-owned	231	19	520	23	1,001	22
	Swedish national	474	39	517	23	1,429	31
	Total for industry	1,218	7	2,270	7	4,641	8

	Value	%	Value	%	Value	%
ISIC 36						
Swedish multinational	252	31	785	58	1,056	52
Foreign-owned	67	8	218	16	88	4
Swedish national	493	61	350	26	873	43
Total for industry	812	4	1,353	4	2,017	3
ISIC 37						
Swedish multinational	2,202	81	3,239	84	3,954	71
Foreign-owned	49	2	113	3	151	3
Swedish national	455	17	507	13	1,457	26
Total for industry	2,706	14	3,859	11	5,562	9
ISIC 38						
Swedish multinational	6,496	76	11,148	72	22,264	74
Foreign-owned	354	4	1,264	8	2,590	9
Swedish national	1,752	20	3,097	20	5,396	18
Total for industry	8,602	44	15,509	45	30,250	48
ISIC 3						
Swedish multinational	11,322	58	20,594	59	37,339	60
Foreign-owned	933	5	2,609	7	4,927	8
Swedish national	7,234	37	11,608	33	20,182	32
Total for companies included	19,489	100	34,811	100	62,448	100
Total Swedish industry	27,418		45,062		83,627	
Share of companies included		71		77		75

Note: To permit comparison over time some data for some, mainly smaller, companies had to be excluded.
The figures do not always add up to subtotals and totals as data for a small number of companies have been excluded.
Source: SOU (1982:15).

OECD report of 1977 indicates that industrial structure in the member countries has experienced a similar pattern of development between 1960 and 1975. None the less, despite a similar pattern of development trends, the OECD countries vary considerably as regards the current status of various industries. The proportion of total industrial production in various industries in a number of countries is indicated in Figure 11.1. The figure indicates that Sweden has relatively limited food and textile industries and that the Swedish chemical industry is also rather insignificant by international standards. On the other hand, as regards the engineering industry, Sweden has the highest proportion of all countries, while Japan, the USA, France, West Germany and Great Britain also achieve high ratings. The Swedish wood, pulp and paper industry is also relatively prominent.

The significance of various industries in different countries can be explained in terms of variations in the environment in which production takes place, which can, in their turn, be due to access to differing production factors or can be traced to historical developments. Historical development may have been due to chance factors to some extent — chance may have determined where industrial manufacturing started and subsequent development may well have been self-generating. The very existence of industrial manufacturing leads to the acquisition of know-how and economies of scale which are a precondition for expansion. This self-generating process, in combination with countries' varying natural endowments, should imply that industrial structure varies even more than it does between different countries. Other factors enter in here, however, to counteract this tendency.

Differences in endowments have the greatest importance for industries closely based on raw materials. As raw materials have become less important in the total industrial picture, it is quite natural that differences between countries become less important as explanatory factors when discussing industrial structure. In the case of production in the rapidly expanding engineering industry, there has been some evening out in terms of technological know-how and price of production factors. This means that production cost has become less important as a reason for localising production to one country or another — instead, the size of the market is a good example of a factor that has become increasingly important. It is thus advantageous to locate production in large countries, with economies of scale, minimal transport costs and close proximity to many customers.

If we develop the arguments presented above, we might propose a hypothesis where international investments contribute to a levelling out

Figure 11.1: Size of Various Industry Sectors in certain OECD Countries in the early 1970s (%)

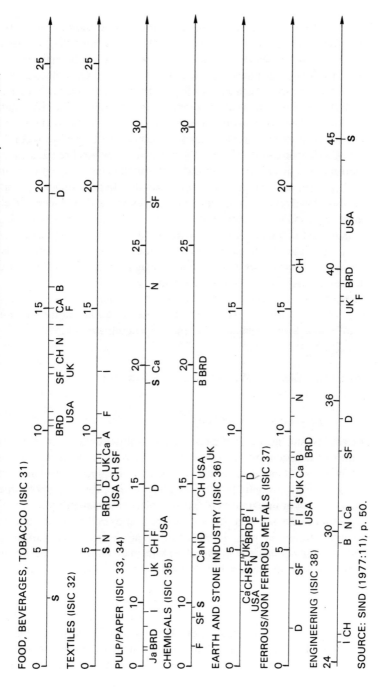

SOURCE: SIND (1977:11), p. 50.

of differences as regards the relative importance of various industries in different countries and this levelling-out process takes place primarily between large countries with markets which are sufficiently extensive to justify local production of most types of products. In the case of small countries operating under free trade conditions, such as Sweden, the industrial structure would be primarily determined by supply-centred localisation factors. A small country tends to have an industrial structure which is determined by natural endowments or by historical factors. Production of other types of goods will not be localised in a small country, but manufactured elsewhere, and then imported by small markets. Set against the background of this hypothesis, it appears somewhat worrying that the centre of gravity in the dominant Swedish engineering industry is in the process of shifting abroad. The result could be industrial stagnation in Sweden, since we cannot count on any major investment input due to the limited size of the market. As noted previously, Swedish industries based on raw materials have experienced a deterioration in their competitive situation and cannot therefore be expected to fill the gap which may occur if the engineering industry does not expand sufficiently. However, this does not mean that the solution is to hinder Swedish companies from expanding abroad.

Structural Changes Within Industries Resulting from Foreign Direct Investments

Concentration and Competition

Direct investments can influence the competitive situation in different industries in various ways. An input of direct investments might increase the number of companies in a given industry in a specific country. On the other hand, in contradiction of this assumption, we should not forget that the input of investments often takes place in a rather different manner — for example where an existing Swedish-owned company is taken over by foreign interests. In this case, the number of companies in the industry will not increase as a result of foreign investments. If the foreign company is newly started, but also large in comparison with local companies in the host country, the long-term result may be that the local companies cannot compete, thus leading to a more concentrated company structure.

In the various sub-industries where major Swedish companies established manufacturing facilities abroad at an early stage, increasing concentration has occurred over time. This tendency towards concentration has been matched by corporate competitive behaviour increasingly based on marketing and technological development. Products have become more complex and differentiated and market demand has not always grown as rapidly as the requisite investments in development and marketing organisations. This has meant that some companies have been eliminated or taken over by others.

When assessing the degree of concentration, it is not sufficient merely to study conditions in individual countries, since global oligopoly applies in industries affected by such concentration. Amongst the industries which we have studied in some detail, telecommunications can be said to have been heavily concentrated for many years. The rock-drill industry has only recently attained its high degree of concentration, while in the welding and ventilation industries, for example, concentration tendencies have progressed relatively little so far.

There are several possible explanations for the fact that company concentration has occurred in differing degrees in the industries studied. There are greater opportunities to achieve company-specific advantages in telecommunications equipment companies than in companies manufacturing welding electrodes. Opportunities for further development of the product vary, as do the potential number of purchasers and variations in their requirements. It should be noted, however, that companies in the ventilation and welding industries are trying to create competitive advantages by expanding their marketing, contracting and service operations and it is not at all impossible that the trend towards more complex product systems may lead to increased company concentration in these industries too.

The fact that horizontal investments in the form of the purchase of existing companies does not have any apparent effect on the company structure, either in the home country or in the host country, may explain why the authorities entrusted with the supervision of competition do not intervene to hinder international acquisitions as they would in the case of domestic acquisitions. Another important explanation in this context is that there is no international organ responsible for supervising international competition. Thus Electrolux, despite its role as one of the world's two or three major manufacturers of vacuum cleaners, was allowed to purchase the American vacuum cleaner company, NUE. In contrast, the American authorities would not have allowed Hoover, Electrolux's American competitor to purchase NUE.

Studies at both company and industrial sector levels have indicated that foreign manufacturing is on the increase, while the company structure in various sub-industries is becoming more concentrated on a global scale. In the case of individual countries, however, it may be difficult to determine whether direct investments lead to a more concentrated company structure.[1] We are faced, once again, with the question of what would have happened if foreign investments had been less extensive. An alternative situation, which is unfortunately less realistic, might be that foreign sales would have been based on manufacture in Sweden to a greater extent. Assuming that export companies could have paid sufficiently high wages and obtained the additional labour which this alternative would have required, company structure would have been more concentrated than it is today.

The alternative situation is that companies would have chosen to diversify in Sweden instead (i.e. expanded in new product areas for manufacturing and sales within Sweden). If this strategy had succeeded, in competition with existing Swedish and foreign companies, the result could have been a less concentrated company structure at the industry level and a higher degree of Swedish self-sufficiency.

Both these alternative situations are, however, extremely hypothetical and if we wish to discuss effects on the structure of industry we must carefully specify conditions for the comparative alternative in order to make any kind of statement with some degree of certainty. Current conditions favour development within the existing product field on an international basis so very clearly that it is difficult to imagine any other realistic alternative.

The hypothesis that direct investments lead to increased concentration, above all in an international perspective, can be attacked, however. Major changes, above all of a technological nature, can change the situation and make it possible for 'new' companies to surmount barriers to entry. Developments within the telecommunications equipment industry may provide an appropriate example.

Organisation of Production Activities

Our case studies and studies of industrial sectors indicate that the companies examined had dropped certain types of manufacturing and had placed increasing emphasis on marketing, in a broad sense. The increased importance of the marketing function can be explained in terms of increasing attention paid by companies to solving buyer problems by offering what are known as system packages, where several products may be combined or adapted to meet specific purchaser requirements. Systems sales do not mean, however, that components included in the final product are more differentiated, but rather that the reverse is more likely to be the case. The central feature of systems sales is that both the seller and the buyer can achieve mutual advantages if products, and above all components, are standardised. The purchaser's specific requirements can then be met by means of various combinations of standard items.

This increased standardisation has meant that a single component manufacturer can supply several companies responsible for systems sales. As systems sales develop, companies responsible for such sales tend to stop manufacturing some of the more simple components used in the system. Manufacturing cost is probably the decisive factor in determining who is to manufacture components and manufacturing cost, in turn, is closely linked to the volume of the production run. This fits the empirical observation that many components are manufactured by companies located in major countries, such as West Germany. Companies in such countries probably have a time lead in terms of the creation of manufacturing capacity which, for example, Swedish component manufacturers may have difficulty in meeting. There is therefore some reason to fear that Sweden is in the process of becoming an 'assembly plant'.

Furthermore, we are not only faced with a shift forwards in the production chain, tending to eliminate the manufacture of some of the more simple components, but we can also observe increased specialisation of the various production units within multinational companies. The clearest example here is the specialisation which has developed between SKF's various subsidiaries in the EEC. In other industries, such as the clothing industry, certain production processes have been located in countries offering advantageous production conditions. In some cases, this type of specialisation may lead to contracting out manufacturing operations to independent companies who thus become subcontractors. These observations are compatible with the trend noted by OECD (1981) where we find traditional multinational companies transforming themselves into international organisations responsible for research and development, marketing and the coordination of these functions with manufacture by independent companies. Developments in this direction would have far-reaching consequences for countries wishing to influence their own international competitiveness.

The Effects of Foreign Investments on the Structure of Other Industries

The developments leading to larger and more internationalised companies do not only affect the structure of the industry directly concerned. Changes in one industry may also have indirect effects on another industry. The consequences of increased concentration in the retail trade on the clothing and furniture industries are examples of such indirect effects which we have found in our studies. Certain changes in the structure of the furniture industry can be largely ascribed to the establishment of IKEA and its expansion, especially abroad.

The structure of the buyer's industry may also be affected by multinational suppliers, who may develop and deliver new machines which permit increased realisation of economies of scale or otherwise change the production situation. An example here might be the latest generation of public telephone exchanges, where increased handling capacity has reduced the number of operational exchanges required. However, this type of structural change can only be explained by the effects of foreign direct investments to a very limited extent.

Summary

The most rapid growth has occurred in industries with extensive foreign investments and products which have required a heavy input of technological staff and research and development. In the overall perspective, companies operating at an international level represent an increasing proportion of the output of Swedish industry. International companies have increased their market shares in growth industries and reduced their shares in stagnant industries.

Our studies at the company and industrial sector levels indicate that the company structure in industries with extensive direct investments has become increasingly concentrated from a global point of view. Products in these industries have become more differentiated and, since market demand has not always grown as rapidly as essential investments in development and marketing organisations, some companies have been eliminated or taken over by others, thus increasing the degree of concentration.

In the companies and sectors studied, systems sales have played an increasingly important role. Systems sales involve standardisation of products and, above all, of components while buyer's differing requirements are met by varying combinations of standard units. To an increasing extent, Swedish multinationals have stopped manufacturing relatively simple components themselves and have instead concentrated on the manufacture of key elements of the final product and on assembly. Some multinational companies have also pursued a policy of specialisation where various European production companies have been assigned areas of special competence.

Conclusions from the Empirical Studies in Part Two

Two main methods have been used to obtain the empirical results which we have described. One method has involved the study of individual companies and specific direct investments. This method has given us answers to questions such as: What were the reasons behind this direct investment? What would have happened — to the company and its intermediate environment — if this particular investment had not taken place and everything else had remained unchanged? Information about the effects in specific cases cannot, however, be automatically expressed in terms of statements about the collective effect of investments on the national economy. This is an inevitable problem with this method and, in principle, we would still have been faced with the same difficulties if we had studied every single investment which had ever been made.

The other method used in our studies has involved statistical description of direct investments and of companies making such investments. This method has given us answers to questions such as: What kind of a correlation do we have between direct investments and variables such as exports, employment and technological development? What differences are there between multinational and national companies as regards growth, efficiency, exports, etc? The problem in translating the answers to these questions into economic effects is that the cause and effect relationship is complicated. This means that it is impossible to state, without qualification, that direct investments have caused any of the differences which are noted. It is rather a question of mutual correlations between several factors, where direct investments only represent one factor.

Thus we cannot, using empirical data, *directly* answer the most interesting questions: What would have happened to Swedish industry if the level of foreign production had been different? What is going to happen to Swedish industry if foreign investments grow at their current rate? Furthermore, it is not possible to make statements in simple terms about which effects are positive and which negative. The assessment of effects depends, for example, on what is regarded as short-term or long-term and whether we are concerned with multinational groups of companies as a whole or simply the activities of such multinational groups in Sweden. If we are to make some total assessment of the effects, we are forced, instead, to study whether direct investments by companies have led to optimal utilisation of the country's production resources.

Large-scale operations, achieved through international specialisation and product differentiation, have become an increasingly important feature of the economic system. The increasing scale of operations is based, among other things, on an ever increasing emphasis on technological development and marketing by companies. These investments in development and marketing have achieved company-specific advantages which have made it possible, and usually also advantageous and essential, to sell on markets which are considerably larger than the Swedish market. International sales have become essential in order to generate resources for continued development which, it is hoped, will enable Swedish companies to keep up with their competitors. Increased scale of operations and internationalisation have developed in parallel with a trend towards increased concentration and we have to look at the localisation of production activities against this background. Many countries apply some form of trade barrier to imports. In addition, it is often found to be advantageous to manufacture locally so as to be able to establish relationships with buyers — this applies, above all, to investments in the capital goods industries which represent the dominant share of Sweden industry's foreign investments. Furthermore, a substantial and growing proportion of foreign investments have occurred in the form of the purchase of companies where the aim is to attain company-specific advantages rather than to exploit existing advantages. In some cases, however, the main reason for investing abroad has been to reduce manufacturing costs — for example the sewing of clothing in low-wage countries. Marketing reasons, however, lay behind most foreign investments. Unfortunately, it is difficult to classify investments unambiguously and difficulties in achieving an adequate classification are detrimental to any analysis of effects and a possible differentiation of government policy in respect of direct investments.

Our case and industrial sector studies indicate that the outflow of direct investments has led to more favourable development in the Swedish operations of Swedish multinationals than would have been the case if these investments had not taken place. Naturally, the short-term effects on exports and employment are difficult to classify in an unambiguous manner but, in a broader perspective, direct investments have meant that new company-specific advantages have been acquired or established. Increased sales have permitted higher levels of investment in functions which strengthen the company's competitive position. This improvement of competitiveness has benefited the home-based operations of Swedish multinationals considerably in most cases.

Investments by foreign interests in Sweden, like Swedish investments abroad have increasingly taken the form of acquisitions. It is difficult to state, in general terms, to what extent the long-term economic effects of such foreign investments in Sweden are positive or negative — this largely depends on whether the Swedish subsidiaries have been given the resources and freedom of action to develop their competitive strength. The available data for the development of foreign-owned companies are not inconsistent with the hope that foreign-owned companies can realise such opportunities in practice.

One way of answering the question as to whether the effects of direct investments and the resultant repositioning of companies in their respective industries have had positive economic results is to see whether Sweden's comparative advantages have been exploited more effectively than what otherwise would have been the case. Sweden has a strong comparative advantage in the field of production which makes intensive use of human capital (i.e. manufacturing which requires a well-trained and skilled workforce). Other highly developed industrialised countries share this advantage, but in Sweden the advantage is a particularly powerful argument since the country enjoys a relatively even wage and salary structure from the international point of view. Engineering is an example of an industry with a high proportion of skilled labour involved in production — this industry has become proportionately more significant and largely consists of multinational companies. The structure of Swedish industry is, however, the result of a long historical process where foreign direct investments are one influential factor. Thus the structural effects can be said to be wider-ranging and more comprehensive and thus difficult to relate purely to direct investments. If foreign investments had not taken place at all, however, it is likely that the structure of Swedish industry would have been very different and there would have been a lower degree of specialisation.

The value of comparative advantages is not constant but may change as a result of the behaviour of governments, companies or other parties. If foreign direct investments mean that functions which tend to develop and improve competitiveness, functions in which skilled and highly trained personnel are heavily involved, are relocated abroad, Sweden's strong comparative advantage will be influenced. Localisation of these key functions to other countries has not taken place to any great extent, however. Nonetheless, the fact that an increasing proportion of the output of major industrial companies takes place abroad inevitably creates some anxiety about future developments.

Notes

1. Indeed it is difficult to determine the development of the degree of concentration if one attempts to distinguish each area of need (i.e. products which actually or potentially compete with each other).

12 POLICY OPTIONS AND RECOMMENDATIONS

This chapter will briefly summarise the effects of corporative direct investments which we have estimated and then proceed from this background to discuss appropriate alternative courses of action which can be applied at a political level. We conclude by making some recommendations, based on the evaluations of the Swedish position, which we consider to be relatively generally applicable.

Summary and Comments on the Results

The effects which we have assessed can be expressed in a simplified form as follows:

1. Direct investments have favoured technological development in Sweden. Certain groups of companies with a large share of their activities abroad have, however, located some of their research and development operations outside Sweden.

2. The establishment and development of foreign manufacturing abroad has generally strengthened the competitive position of the Swedish multinationals and of their Swedish-based operations.

3. The short-term effects on exports from Sweden vary — they have sometimes been positive, sometimes negative: the improved competitive position resulting from direct investments has, however, had favourable long-term effects on exports.

4. The effects on employment are analogous with the export effects (i.e. a higher level of employment can be achieved for a given cost structure) although the effects on employment may be negative in some cases in the short term. In the long term, the structure of employment is affected in two ways. The multinationals have a high and increasing proportion of salaried employees in the technological development function. Information about the employment structure for wage-earners indicated that the main emphasis in Swedish multinational companies has been in the central, semi-skilled area, while purely national companies employed a high proportion of both skilled and unskilled labour. Foreign-owned companies in Sweden employed the highest proportion of unskilled labour.

5. Direct investments of multinational companies contribute to a

restructuring of Swedish industry in a direction which tends to enhance Sweden's international competitive position.

6. Although we have found that the effects of investments have generally proved positive, this does not imply that each individual investment has had positive effects: investments which lead to a reallocation abroad of corporative functions designed to develop the company's competitive position (e.g. management, research and development, sophisticated manufacturing and central marketing) can lead to a deterioration of the competitive strengths of Swedish-based operations within the group.

If we turn to the effects of the direct investment inflow into Sweden, we do not find any support for the view that foreign-owned companies are characterised by inferior development patterns. In fact, the studies of newly established foreign-owned companies which we have undertaken would tend to contradict this view. The question of whether a foreign acquisition of a Swedish-owned company should be seen as positive or negative depends on whether the new owners permit their Swedish subsidiary to maintain and develop vital corporative functions in Sweden, thus enabling the subsidiary to improve its competitive position.

The growth of major international companies has meant that the company structure has become more concentrated and that greater demands have been placed on regional policy. Both concentration and regional aspects can be seen as negative, from certain points of view. At the same time, however, both tendencies are more or less natural consequences of an ambition to increase economic growth. Much the same can also be said as regards reduced limitations on action when considering the opportunities for pursuing independent economic policies in specific areas. It is therefore scarcely surprising that international companies exploit national differences to their own advantage. However, this also reduces the opportunities for an individual country to pursue policies which companies regard as less than advantageous, compared to other countries. This reduced freedom of action not only has effects on economic policy but also affects national organisations which may find it difficult to cope with the major international companies. However, as regards national freedom of action, the influence of direct investments is marginal providing that exports and imports can move freely across frontiers.

A central question with future relevance is whether Sweden can rely on a sufficiently high and sophisticated level of industrial activity to be able to offer an attractive standard of living, based on goods manufactured in Sweden or purchased from abroad. The answer to this question depends on subjective beliefs about Sweden's attractiveness or appropriateness for industrial activities. The industrial environment, in a broad sense, will have considerable relevance in determining how much corporative investment Sweden receives, irrespective of whether the companies are Swedish multinationals, Swedish nationals or foreign-owned. In this context, the size of the market is also a factor which affects localisation.

Changes in external conditions will mean that some industrial sectors in one country will expand, while in another country they will stagnate. It is more important to remember that such structural changes can only be partially explained in terms of direct investments. In the last decade, companies in industries such as shipbuilding, commercial-grade steel and clothing have encountered a series of reverses, not only in Sweden but in most other West European countries. Yet, as regards at least shipbuilding and steel, there are hardly any multinational companies in these industries. An important factor in the decline of these industries is, instead, that new national companies in Japan, South-East Asia and Latin America have gained significant market shares through exports. We can thus say that, irrespective of whether Swedish companies invest abroad or not, the size of Swedish industry will be largely determined by how well Sweden can compete with foreign manufacturers.

If we now turn to the development of direct investments, we are faced with the important question of what consequences will result from the fact that the foreign production of Swedish companies is increasing, in the long term, more rapidly than their production in Sweden. To some extent, this increase is due to the establishment of new companies with foreign manufacturing facilities, but existing multinationals are also expanding the proportion of their manufacturing outside Sweden. In 1978, four Swedish groups manufactured more than 60 per cent of their output abroad. In other words, these companies had the centre of gravity of their activities outside Sweden. We should therefore not ignore the potential risk that functions which are the key to the company's competitive situation may ultimately be relocated abroad. Apart from the fact that a relocation of this type would make such companies less amenable to influence from Swedish interests, it is also likely that there would be negative economic and industrial effects. This is not primarily a question of existing Swedish manufacturing operations being moved abroad, but rather the risk that industrial renewal and growth in Sweden will not take place, but will instead occur in association with foreign-based operations.

Continued growth of large Swedish multinationals means increasing dependence on such companies. Furthermore, the concentration of decision-making power which inevitably follows from such growth gives rise to some doubts. We are thus faced with a potential dilemma — how can international competitive strength, which leads to increasingly large companies in relation to the Swedish market, be combined with requirements of industrial comprehensiveness, a reduction in economic vulnerability and the avoidance of power concentrations?

Irrespective of how the total effects of international investments are assessed, there is no doubt that these effects have become a significant factor in Swedish industry. This implies that the activities of multinational companies are of considerable interest to society at large and that their continued development must, of course, be studied in various ways. The experience gained in our studies indicated, however, that we cannot rely on obtaining an adequate basis for economic decisions by simply studying individual cases of direct investment. Even where there is, for example, reason to assume that a specific investment has positive effects on exports and employment in Sweden, the underlying industrial effects will not be revealed unless the investment is regarded as a phase in the company's long-term development. These underlying effects may consist of changes in the size of the industrial sector or they may express changes in industrial production resulting from a reduction in manufacturing operations in the company's own plant, an increased level of specialisation, changes in subcontracting systems and the localisation of strategic corporate functions abroad.

Policy Options

The above summary has indicated that the effects of foreign investments are positive, on the whole. But it is also clear that future developments give rise to some anxiety. What is already good can also become better and therefore there are considerable justifications for discussing various alternatives for legislative action.

We assume that economic growth, as in the past, is the primary goal for economic policy. We further assume continued technological development, international specialisation and an increased scale of operation. Our discussion of the policy alternatives is set against this background situation. For reasons that should be obvious at this stage, we intend to concentrate on investment outflows, yet without totally ignoring inflows.

What are the main reasons for attempting to influence investment outflows? We consider that there is a risk that Sweden will be impoverished, in the industrial sphere — that Sweden will become a peripheral factor in the industrialised world. Sweden's limited size and geographical distance from the major markets are disadvantageous. As a result, companies tend to locate their activities abroad. Unfortunately, it is extremely difficult to counteract Sweden's disadvantages but the mechanisms described in the following may, in principle, have some relevance. We should make it clear that we are not primarily interested in ensuring that the 'typical' foreign investment takes place, instead, in Sweden. Rather, we are interested in seeing that Sweden retains investments which involve the relocation of central operations which serve to improve the corporate competitive position which may be regarded as the technology elements in the packages of goods and services marketed by companies. To some extent, however, the relocation of these central operations depends on where the corporate group has already localised other activities. This implies that other investments, primarily in manufacturing capacity, are of some interest too.

In the Swedish case, control over direct investment outflows is mainly exercised by means of currency regulations. This form of regulation assumes that what is to be controlled and influenced is investment financed by capital which has either been exported from the home country or is borrowed by the parent company abroad. Currency regulations could be characterised as a *direct* method of influencing company investments. It is also possible, however, to consider *indirect* methods which instead influence the background to corporate foreign investments — and some examples of such methods will be discussed later.

Currency Regulations

The original reason for the establishment of currency regulations was to influence the balance of foreign payments. Although direct investments represent only a small proportion of the total capital flow across frontiers, Swedish currency regulations require companies to obtain permission to transfer capital out of the country. Permission is also required for a Swedish company to guarantee a loan borrowed in the name of a foreign subsidiary. Sweden has undertaken, as a signatory to the OECD Capital Liberalisation Code, only to refuse permission for direct investment if it is considered that such an investment will lead to substantial damage to the national interest. If each investment is assessed separately, it is probable that any single investment can be only considered to have such undesirable effects in exceptional circumstances. Prior to 1981, there was a further criterion which stipulated that an investment should be favourable to the foreign exchange balance.

Whether we take the present currency regulations as our starting point or those that applied previously, including the balance of exchange criterion, there seem to be three weaknesses in the system. The first weak point is that certain decisions about the expansion of Swedish companies' foreign subsidiaries are not covered by currency regulations. This applies to investments financed via retained profits,[1] or with capital which the foreign subsidiaries borrow without the participation of the parent company. This means that established multinational companies are able to expand their foreign production and transfer abroad central company functions, such as research and development and management, without being obliged to seek prior approval from the Central Bank of Sweden, the authority responsible for administering currency regulations.

The second problem is that movements of capital have declined in importance as a means of corporate internationalisation. New methods of controlling foreign production without formal ownership of the production unit by a foreign parent company have developed, especially in the last ten tears (Dunning, 1979). Various forms of agreement make it possible to create business relationships which resemble those in a group of companies. This type of agreement has many advantages for the parent company or principal. The financial commitment is reduced and flexibility increased since it is easier to change the type of production and suppliers. It is hardly possible to extend currency regulations to include production agreements with foreign corporations. Every order placed abroad can in fact, in a broad sense, be regarded as a production agreement and it would prove practically impossible to distinguish agreements which are of special interest here.

The third weakness in the present system of controls is that the system is only concerned with individual specific investments. If only a single investment, made by a single company, is studied, it can prove difficult to understand what structural effects may result for Swedish subcontractors or the type of production currently pursued by the Swedish parent company. Furthermore, if currency regulations are to be effective, relevant and unambiguous criteria are required. The problem is, however, that a specific type of investment may have different effects when two different companies faced with different competitive situations and other circumstances are involved. How can such factors be taken into consideration without simultaneously introducing a certain measure of subjective judgement? Such a business-oriented scrutiny of direct investments assumes a level of competence which is unlikely to exist in a central bank. All in all, these objections and the problems already mentioned mean that currency regulations must be regarded as an inadequate instrument for influencing foreign direct investments in the national economic interest.

Taxation

A possible way of influencing investments, which has been discussed in the theoretical literature is to tax flows of direct investment (Svedberg, 1977). A tax of this type should have a restricting effect on such investments. There are several objections, however. The first difficulty is that it is not desirable to restrict all types of foreign investment — in fact, many small companies need to be encouraged in their internationalisation process. Furthermore, it is quite feasible to avoid taxation, as is the case with the application of foreign currency regulations, by internationalising corporate operations without formal ownership. This is perhaps an opportunity which is primarily of interest to companies which have already internationalised their organisations to a great extent. Taxation of investment outflows would therefore probably only lead to the introduction of increased taxation pressures but would not achieve the desired effects on the form of steering real development.

Other Legislation Which Directly Regulates Foreign Direct Investments

Investment by Swedish companies in South Africa is prohibited and is one aspect of efforts to put pressure on the South African government. In order to ensure that the prohibition also applies to Swedish multinationals already established in South Africa, the law has been directed at company management in Sweden who, on pain of punishment in the event of an adverse judgement in the courts, are obliged to ensure that subsidiaries do not invest. Special permission can be sought for investments required to replace existing assets.

Similar constructions could be used for other forms of investment outflows, at least theoretically. What is not considered desirable can be prohibited — this might involve all types of investment, investments in certain industries or countries, investments by certain Swedish companies or investments which lead to shifts in the share of activities (in the form of production, value added, etc., or certain values established for multinationals as a whole). Legislation of this type would also allow possibilities for special permission on application.

One problem with the methods suggested above is, however, that it would probable be difficult to demarcate investments to be covered by the law. The main objection is, however, that it is of course not at all certain that corresponding investments would, instead, take place in Sweden. It is quite possible that no investment at all would be carried out or that collaboration would be established with an independent company abroad. It is therefore unlikely that this form of legislation would be especially successful either.

International Agreements

One reason that Swedish companies invest abroad is that many countries demand, require or favour local manufacturing in various ways. An indirect method of achieving reduced foreign investments would therefore be to attempt to reach agreements whereby countries would not require or favour local production but would instead accept free trade (Niehans, 1977).

Many initiated observers, however, believe that requirements favouring local manufacturing will tend to increase rather than be reduced. One reason for this development is that the continuing structural change process in many countries' economies is tending to become increasingly difficult. The costs for industrial transformation are increasing, while the ability to adapt appears to be diminishing. Many developing countries favour local production, in view of their difficult foreign exchange situation. If protectionism increases and the favourisation of local manufacturing increases, it will become more desirable, especially for the smaller countries, to try to achieve international agreements to hinder such developments.

A further problem which requires international cooperation is the question of whether current corporate concentration trends lead to improper limitations on competition. As things are now, each country decides individually to what extent the effects of corporate mergers in the country should be limited while mergers between companies in different countries lie outside such regulatory systems.

Thus, we may observe that international agreements should be able to create a basis for increased global economic well-being. The actual possibilities of achieving results in this direction should not be overestimated. At the root of the problem lie national antagonisms and the country which can succeed in outbidding the others or permit its corporations to monopolise world markets can show a profit. Such policies tend to lead to imitation and some countries ultimately risk winding up in a worse situation than they started off with.

Influencing the Industrial Environment

Another indirect method of dealing with problems which can result from foreign investments is to improve the infrastructural preconditions for investments in the home country by taking appropriate measures. Where it is possible to create good conditions for investments within the home country, there are excellent opportunities for dealing with two problems: the decline of the industrial sector and the reallocation of certain corporate central functions. Industrial size in Sweden is not only dependent on the extent of direct foreign investments. The total investment volume in Sweden can, in fact, be increased by stimulating both multinational and national companies to expand in Sweden.

The second problem, involving a risk that central functions are relocated to foreign sections of the company, could probably also be reduced by applying the appropriate measures, such as investment in education, training and research and also investments in the infrastructure in areas such as communications and environmental conservation. There is considerable evidence that these types of activity are of importance for industrial renewal and development.

Influencing Corporate Objectives

Companies invest abroad for rational reasons — because foreign investment is considered the most advantageous alternative. In such an evaluation process, the domestic economic situation and the national interest are not relevant dimensions for companies. The question is therefore whether it might not be possible to reduce the risk of industrial stagnation in the home country and relocation of important corporate functions abroad by influencing the company's goals in some way so that management take the economic effects of their actions in the home country into account to a greater extent. Two points of view should be considered in this connection. The first is what consequences would such a modification of objectives have on the company's competitive position.[2] If there is little difference between the alternatives in terms of advantage to the company — for example between investing abroad or at home — selecting the next best alternative might in some cases only marginally weaken the company's competitive position. The other side of the picture then becomes how it would then be possible to introduce the idea of greater consideration for the national interest. One way of influencing a company's goal functions would be to try to influence corporate decisions from the inside by means of owner influence or board representation. Another way would be by means of some form of influence on attitudes, which would then lead to a more active search process for domestic investment alternatives on the part of company management.

The discussion around this method of influencing direct investments has assumed that there is a margin available on certain investments within which the company can choose between locating an investment either abroad or in the home country. If there is no margin, however, the less advantageous alternative will weaken the company's competitive position and the risk that existing operations in the home country may suffer cannot be ignored. We do not believe that it is possible to base a policy on assessment of whether there are such reserve margins or not. Only the management of the specific company involved are in a position to make such an assessment with any degree of certainty.

Discussions Between the Government and Major Companies

By this stage, it should be clear that direct methods for influencing direct investments are unlikely to be particularly effective. Furthermore, it is difficult to accept the effectiveness of the indirect methods since we require further information about factors in the industrial environment which tend to determine corporate investment and localisation decisions. However, a limited number of companies are responsible for the major proportion of Swedish industry's manufacturing and investments abroad. It therefore seems reasonable that attention should be primarily directed towards these few companies. This might take place in the form of an information system which permits a continuing dialogue between the state and major Swedish corporate groups.

The object of such discussions should be that the companies and the government mutually inform and influence each other. The state needs better information, in a qualitative sense, about the conditions faced by corporations, while companies need to know more about governmental intentions. On the government side, the objective may be said to be to inform industry about the development of Swedish economic policy as it affects company objectives. This should stimulate companies to take Swedish economic policy into consideration. On the other hand, companies would be able to transmit to the government information as to how they regard their investment and competitive situations in the long term, both in Sweden and internationally, and they may indicate what action might facilitate industrial renewal.

The discussion system sketched out above should form part of a long-term industrial strategy for Sweden, in which the localisation of new major investments is assumed to be an important factor. Thus, foreign investments should not be treated in isolation but should be seen in correlation with overall corporate strategy alternatives, including total investment operations. A systematic dialogue could prove to be a selective instrument which allowed consideration for the fact that companies are faced with varying situations which lead to varying requirements to be taken into account. The companies' ability 'to take economic policy into consideration' when considering localisation of investments is therefore also likely to vary.

Operations which have already been internationalised to a considerable degree can only be influenced marginally. Major interest centres rather on new production areas and industries which are still in the relatively early stages of the product life-cycle. The limited size of the Swedish market is a strong argument for limiting the sphere of attention in this way. New activities, based in Sweden, must be created. In this connection, for example, areas which have been allocated political priority can be linked to corporate know-how (e.g. new public transport systems). In addition, it should prove possible to find gaps in the industrial networks (i.e. where certain components are not currently manufactured in Sweden) and attempt to initiate production to fill the gap or alternatively to attempt to persuade a foreign company to establish a plant in Sweden.

It should be possible to limit the discussion system described above to include only major companies. As an example, we may mention that the 20 largest companies in Sweden represent approximately three quarters of Swedish industry's foreign output. In 1978, these 20 companies represented no less than 56 per cent of industrial research and development, 36 per cent of exports and 30 per cent of industrial employment in Sweden.

The great advantage of the discussion system is that it places direct investments in a context where they belong from point of view of economic policy — as an element in the total development of the company. The discussion system also permits the selective assessment of investments. The system may, however, involve the risk that industrial policy focuses on the problems of the major companies at the expense of small companies. Another objection to a discussion system, which is often voiced, is that it involves a step towards an economy which is increasingly based on negotiation processes. On the other hand, it might be said that a discussion system could well mean that negotiations which already have taken place *de facto* receive clearer recognition and appropriate political rules. An objection which we regard as decisive, however, is that politicians might attempt to influence companies directly — this would be highly unfortunate.

International Law and Sweden's International Commitments

The restrictions which Sweden has taken upon itself in the form of participation in international cooperation and the signing of international conventions are an important aspect in any assessment of the applicability of the methods discussed so far. Since some of the methods that have been presented may conflict with Sweden's international commitments, these problems are briefly considered below. International law, regulating the mutual relationships of countries, has, to some extent, the character of customary law. However, where international legal aspects are covered by the UN Charter, international law takes on a more codified colouring. An example of the codification of international law is the right of a country to exercise jurisdiction over its own territories and, as a result, the absence of any such rights as regards the exercise of jurisdiction over other countries' territories. This aspect is of interest in view of the opportunities which legislation presents to influence corporate expansion abroad.

An example of this type of legislative regulation is the law prohibiting Swedish investments in South Africa. In this case, legislation was not considered sufficiently effective to regulate actual movements of capital (SOU, 1978:53). Fewer than 10 per cent of Swedish-owned subsidiaries in South Africa covered their investment financing requirements in the period 1970–6 by means of transfers fron Sweden (SOU, 1978:53, p. 158). It was therefore decided to prohibit totally all investments in South Africa. Since the Swedish subsidiaries are South African enterprises from the legal point of view, the law is directed at Swedish management at corporate group level who are then held responsible for ensuring that Swedish subsidiaries do not undertake investments which are contrary to Swedish law.

This state of affairs may be considered an indirect means of intruding in South African jurisdiction since Swedish group management is required to influence the boards and managements of South African companies. This was certainly the case presented by members of the South African Committee who reserved judgement and similar views were expressed in critical submissions to the Committee (Swedish Riksdag Bill 1978/79:196). In some cases the critics based their views on studies undertaken by internationally recognised experts in international law.

The Committee which examined the South African Bill considered, however, that if the proposed statute came into conflict with South African law, then South African law should apply and that therefore there was no conflict with the principles of international laws. The majority

of the South African Committee and the government accepted this.
The so-called 'Höganäs' conditions' which have to be accepted if the
Central Bank of Sweden is to permit the transfer of funds for direct investment also have extraterritorial implications. Under the terms of the
Höganäs conditions Swedish-owned foreign subsidiaries must remit their
profits (in excess of what is required for normal consolidation) to Sweden
and, furthermore, such subsidiaries are not permitted, in their turn, to
form subsidiaries. Thus, the Höganäs agreement in effect applies to
foreign legal entities. As far as is known, however, there has been no
discussion, either in Sweden or internationally, about the Höganäs
conditions.

We are not competent to form our own judgement as to what international law permits in this case. It is none the less possible that the
assessments that have been made to date have been influenced by the
fact that South Africa was involved — a country ruled by a widely
detested regime (see Swedish Riksdag Bill 1978/79:116). The assessments
— and in any case the risk of counteraction — would almost certainly
be different when considering a law which had similar indirect effects,
universally, on all other countries.

The international commitment which primarily limits opportunities
to prevent or restrict direct investment outflows is the OECD Capital
Liberalization Code. The signatories of the Code have undertaken not
to set up barriers limiting international capital movements and direct investments are included under this heading.[2] Direct investments may only
be hindered in special cases, specifically detailed in so-called 'statutory
notes'. As has been mentioned previously, the Swedish Currency Board
applies two criteria at present: that an investment must not harm the country's interests to any exceptional degree and that a certain proportion
of investments must be financed abroad. In other respects, Sweden's position as a signatory of the Code means that we have undertaken not to
hinder direct investment outflows.

Recommendations

Our coverage of various methods for influencing direct investments indicates that no single method fulfils all requirements. We therefore recom-
mend that government policy in respect of direct investments utilises
several methods which complement each other.

In our opinion a reinforcement of the industrial infrastructure (i.e.

the educational system and basic research) is a central factor in attempting to influence corporate investments. Furthermore, an improved infrastructure has effects on all categories of companies, including foreign-owned and national corporations and thus complies, to a great extent, with methods which may be used to stimulate national economic growth.

Current currency regulations and rules for detailed applications of the regulations, which give the Central Bank of Sweden the right to refuse permission for capital exports where a direct investment can damage the national interest seriously from the point of view of employment or industrial policy, probably have no practical significance. However, currency regulation continues to have some political relevance and is therefore likely to be retained.

Regulations and action taken by authorities in other countries also influence corporate localisation decisions. It is therefore important that Sweden attempts to achieve harmonisation in this area, for example by exerting its influence in organisations devoted to international cooperation, such as the OECD. If such efforts do not prove successful, there is a risk that competition will be distorted. A further factor which threatens competition is the increasing corporate concentration, both in Sweden and internationally, which characterises certain industries. We therefore consider it desirable that international cooperation is intensified in the field of supervision of competition. An appropriate form for such supervision might be via the Centre on Transnational Corporations, established by the United Nations, which has, among other things, collected and processed data about multinational companies. We assume that Sweden will continue to participate in the further development of the codes of behaviour which have already been agreed (for example, within the OECD) or which are currently under discussion (for example, by the UN).

It is probably clear at this stage that we are not very impressed by the idea of attempting to influence direct investments on a case-by-case basis. Having studied the development processes in a number of companies, we consider that it is pointless to attempt to assess the effects in advance. General, indirect methods are to be preferred. It is not feasible to regulate foreign investments directly in a successful manner since there are so many other opportunities for internationalisation which remain open.

Pursuing a long-term economic policy which favoured growth would probably also increase the inflow of investments into Sweden — the problem with such inflows is that they are too limited. There is a need to disseminate information to foreign companies about the conditions for pursuing industrial or other business activities in Sweden. Indeed, the Swedish Ministry of Industry has recently prepared a brochure with this objective in mind. It is, however, scarcely likely that Sweden will ever achieve a perfect balance between investment inflows and outflows — the market is too small and the shortage of skilled and well-trained labour is too great.

Notes

1. Profits over and above what is required for normal consolidation should be transferred to the parent company. In practice, however, it is difficult to decide where this limit should be drawn.

2. It may be worthy of mention that Canada, although a member of OECD, has not signed the Capital Liberalisation Code.

BIBLIOGRAPHY

Alvstam, C.G. and Lundin, M. (1983) *Världshandelns geografi*, Sveriges Redarförening, Liber Hermods, Malmö.

Behrman, J.N. (1971) Government Policy Alternatives and the Problem of International Sharing; in Dunning, J.H. (ed.) *The Multinational Enterprise*, London.

Bergsten, C.F., Horst, T. and Moran, T.H. (1978) *American Multinationals and American Interests*, Brookings Institution, Washington DC.

Carlson, S. (1979) *Swedish Industry Goes Abroad*, Lund.

Carlsson, B. (1979) *Teknik och industristruktur — 70-talets ekonomiska kris i historisk belysning*, IUI/IVA, Stockholm.

Carlsson, B. (1980) *Technical Change and Productivity in Swedish Industry in the Post-War Period*, IUI Research Report, 8.

Caves, R.E. (1971) International Corporations: The Industrial Economics of Foreign Investment, *Economica*, 38, pp.1–27.

Corden, W.M. (1974a) The Theory of International Trade; in Dunning, J.H. (ed.) *Economic Analysis and the Multinational Enterprise*, London.

Corden, W.M. (1974b) *Trade Policy and Economic Welfare*, Oxford University Press, Oxford.

DIRK, see SOU '1981:33; 1981:43; 1982:15; 1982:27; 1983:16; 1983:17'.

Dunning, J.H. (1958) *American Investment in British Manufacturing Industry*, Allen and Unwin, London.

Dunning J.H. (1969) The Foreign Investment Controversy, *Bankers Magazine* (May, June, July).

Dunning, J.H. (1979) Recent Developments in Research on Multinational Enterprises: An Economist's Viewpoint; in *Recent Research on the Internationalization of Business*, Almqvist and Wiksell International, Uppsala.

Dunning, J.H. and Pearce, R.D. (1981) *The World's Largest Industrial Enterprises*, Gower, Aldershot.

EFTA (1980) *Bulletin*, 1.

EFTA (1982) *Bulletin*, 2.

Eliasson, G. (1971) *Diagnos på 70-talet*, Stockholm.

Fackföreningsrörelsen och de multinationella företagen (1976) Report to the Congress of Swedish Confederation of Trade Unions, Prisma/LO, Stockholm.

Forsgren, M. and Larsson, A. (1984) Foreign Acquisition and the Balance of Power in Transnational Enterprises: The Swedish Case; Working Paper no. 2, Centre for International Business Studies, Uppsala University.

Frank, R. and Freeman, R. (1978) *Distributional Consequences of Direct Foreign Investment*, New York.

Giersch, H. (1979) *On the Economics of Intra-Industry Trade*, Mohr, Tübingen.

Grubel, H.G. and Lloyd, P.J. (1975) *Intra-Industry Trade*, London.

Hallvarsson, M. (1980) *Industrialismen 100 år*, Industriförbundets Förlag/Veckans Affärer.

Heckscher, E.F. (1936) Industrins historiska förutsättningar och allmänna karaktär, *Sveriges Industri*, Sveriges Industriförbund, Stockholm.

Hennart, J.-F. (1982) *A Theory of Multinational Enterprise*, University of Michigan Press, Ann Arbor.

Hirsch, S. (1976) An International Trade and Investment Theory of the Firm, *Oxford Economic Papers*, 28.

Hood, N. and Young, S. (1979) *The Economics of Multinational Enterprise*, London.

180

Hörnell, E. and Vahlne, J.-E. (1972) *The Deciding Factors in the Choice of a Sales Subsidiary as the Channel for Exports*, Uppsala.
Horst, T. (1973) The Simple Analytics of Multinational Firm Behaviour; in Conolly, M.B. and Swoboda, A.K. (eds.), *International Trade and Money*, pp. 72–84, George Allen and Unwin, London.
How SKF International Keeps a Grip on 18 Currencies (1982) *Euromoney* (September), pp. 341–51.
Hufbauer, G.C. and Adler, F.M. (1968) *Overseas Manufacturing Investment and the Balance of Payments*, US Treasury Dept., Washington DC.
Hymer, S. (1960) The International Operations of National Firms: A Study of Direct Investment; unpubl. diss., MIT.
Information Canada (1970) *Foreign Ownership and The Structure of Canadian Industry*, Report of the Task Force on the Structure of Canadian Industry, Ottawa.
Information Canada (1972) *Foreign Direct Investment in Canada*, Ottawa.
Jungnickel, R. *et al.* (1977) Einfluss multinationaler Unternehmen auf Aussenwirtschaft und Branschenstruktur der Bundesrepublik Deutschland, Verlag Weltarchiv.
Macdoughall, G.D.A. (1960) The Benefits and Costs of Private Investments from Abroad: A Theoretical Approach, *Economic Record*, 36.
Mundell, R.A. (1957) International Trade and Factor Mobility, *American Economic Review*, 47.
Musgrave, P. (1975) *Direct Investments Abroad and the Multinationals: Effects on the United States Economy*, US Government Printing Office, Washington DC.
Niehans, J. (1977) Benefits of Multinational Firms for a Small Parent Economy: The Case of Switzerland; in Agmon, T. and Kindleberger, C.P., *Multinationals from Small Countries*, MIT Press.
Ny lagstiftning om utländska förvärv av svenska företag m.m., Regeringens proposition 1981/2:135, Liber, Stockholm.
OECD (1970) *Gaps in Technology: Analytical Report*, Paris.
OECD (1978) *Survey of Member Country Policies, Procedures and Practices with Regard to International Direct Investment*, Paris.
OECD (1979) *Facing the Future*, Paris.
OECD (1981) *Recent Trends in International Direct Investment*, Paris.
Ohlsson, L. (1980) *Engineering Trade Specialisation of Sweden and Other Industrial Countries*, North Holland, Amsterdam.
Parry, T.G. (1978) Structure and Performance of Australian Manufacturing Industry with Special Reference to Foreign-Owned Enterprises; in Kaspar, W. and Parry, T.G. (eds.) *Growth, Trade and Structural Change in an Open Australian Economy*, Centre for Applied Economic Research.
Parry, T.G. (1980) *The Multinational Enterprise, International Investment and Host Country Impacts*, JAI Press, Greenwich, Conn.
Porter, M.E. (1980) *Competitive Strategy — Techniques for Analysing Industries and Competitors*, The Free Press, London.
Reddaway, W.B. (1968) *Effects of United Kingdom Direct Investment Overseas*, London.
Renber, G.L. *et al.* (1973) *Private Foreign Investment in Development*, Oxford University Press, Oxford.
Rugman, A.M. (1981) *Inside the Multinationals: The Economics of Internal Markets*, Croom Helm, London and Columbia University Press, New York.
Rugman, A.M. (1983) Performance of U.S. and European Multinationals, *Management International Review*, 2, pp. 4–14.
Samuelsson, H.-F. (1977) *Utländska direkta investeringar i Sverige. En ekonomisk analys av bestämningsfaktorerna*, IUI, Stockholm.
Sandén, P. and Vahlne, J.-E. (1976) Impact of Multinationality on Performance; Working Paper, Centre for International Business Studies, University of Uppsala.
SCB (1977:23) *SOS Industri, Forskningsstatistik (1975–77)*, Memorandum Foreign Trade Statistics, Stockholm.

SCB (1978:7) *Export av tjänster (1977)*, Stockholm.
SCB (1980:1) *Export och import av tjänster (1978)*, Stockholm.
SCB (1980:2) *Sveriges internationella företag*, Company Statistics, Stockholm.
SCB (1980:8) *SOS Industristatistik*, Memorandum Industry Statistics, Stockholm.
SIND (1977:10) *Multinationella företag i svensk livsmedelsindustri*, Stockholm.
SIND (1977:11) *Industriutvecklingen i Sverige*, Stockholm.
SIND (1980:4) *Multinationella företag: FOU-verksamhet, tekniköverföring och företagstillväxt*, Stockholm.
SIND (1981:3) *Hur kan konkurrenskraften förbättras?*, Stockholm.
SIND (1982:3) *När kommer krisen? En regional och branschvis analys av den svenska industrins nedläggnings- och förnyelsebehov under 1980-talet*, Stockholm.
Solomon, L.D. (1978) *Multinational Corporations and the Emerging World Order*, Kennikat Press Corp.
SOU (1975:50) *Internationella koncerner i industriländer — samhällsekonomiska — aspekter*, Report of the Committee on Concentration of Economic Power, Liber, Stockholm.
SOU (1978:53) *Förbud mot svenska investeringar i Sydafrika*, Liber, Stockholm.
SOU (1978:73) *Kontroll av utländsk företagsetablering i Sverige m.m.*, Report of the Committee on Foreign Take-Overs of Swedish Companies, Liber, Stockholm.
SOU (1981:33) *Effekter av investeringar utomlands*, Report of the Committee on Foreign Direct Investment (DIRK), Liber, Stockholm.
SOU (1981:43) *De internationella investeringarnas effekter*, Report of the Committee on Foreign Direct Investment, Liber, Stockholm.
SOU (1982:15) *Internationella företag i svensk industri*, Report of the Committee on Foreign Direct Investment, Liber, Stockholm.
SOU (1982:27) *Svensk industri i utlandet*, Report of the Committee on Foreign Direct Investment, Liber, Stockholm. Also published as Swedenborg, B. (1982) *Svensk industrie i utlandet*, Industrins utrechningsinstitut, Stockholm.
SOU (1983:16) *Sysselsättningsstrukturen i internationella företag*, Report of the Committee on Foreign Direct Investment, Liber, Stockholm.
SOU (1983:17) *Näringspolitiska effekter av internationella investeringar*, Final Report of the Committee on Foreign Direct Investment, Liber, Stockholm.
SOU (1984:6) *De utlandsetablerade företagen och den svenska ekonomin*, Bilagedel 2, Särskilda studier, Liber, Stockholm.
Stobaugh, R.B. (1971) The Multinational Corporation: Measuring the Consequences, *Columbia Journal of World Business* (January/February).
Svedberg, P. (1977) *Foreign Investment and Trade Policies*, Stockholm.
Sveriges 3.000 största företag 1982 (1982) Liber, Malmö.
Swedenborg, B. (1973) *Den svenska industrins investeringar i utlandet*, Industrins Utredningsinstitut, Stockholm.
Swedish Ministry of Industrial Policy (1980:17) *Att utveckla en långsiktig industripolitik*, Report of the Information for Industrial Policy Committee, Liber, Stockholm.
UN Department of Economic and Social Affairs (1973) *Multinational Corporations in World Development* (ST/ECA/190).
UN Economic and Social Council (1978) *Transnational Corporations in World Development*, New York.
US Tariff Commission (1973) *Implications of Multinational Firms for World Trade and Investment and for US Trade and Labor*, Report to the Committee on Finance of the United States Senate and its Subcommittee on International Trade, US Government Printing Office, Washington DC.
Van den Bulcke, D. and Halsberghe, E. (1979) *Effects of Multinational Enterprises on Employment*, ILO, Geneva.
Vaupel, J.V. (1971) *Characteristics and Motivation of the US Corporations that Manufacture Abroad*, mimeographed, Cambridge.

Veckans affärer (1984:16) Färre jobb utomlands i svenska multisar, pp. 50–5, Stockholm.

Veckans affärer (1984:17) Storföretagen nära 1974 års vinstnivå, p. 50, Stockholm.

Verkstadsindustrins konjunkturläge (1984:2) Sveriges Mekanförbund and Sveriges Verkstadsförening, Stockholm.

Wohlert, K. (1981) *Framväxten av svenska multinationella företag*, Uppsala.

APPENDIX A: THE 20 LARGEST SWEDISH MULTINATIONALS (1983)

Company logotype and name	Employees abroad Number	Percentage of total	Foreign in relation to total sales (%)	Main products (estimated share in world market)
AGA	7,662	68	69	Industrial Gases, Welding Equipment, Cold Storage, Freezing Equipment.
Alfa Laval	10,352	65	90	Centrifugal Separators (30–50%), Compact Heat Exchangers (30–50%) Milking Machines (30–50%).
ASEA (excl. Fläkt)	11,582	27	65	Equipment for Distribution of Electric Power, Energy Generation Equipment.
Astra	3,206	51	80	Seloken (17%), Xylocain (40%), Bricanyl (10%).
Atlas Copco	11,996	71	91	Airpower, Mining and Construction Technique.

Company		Description
Electrolux	58,372	66	76	Electrical Domestic Appliances, Metals, Various Industrial Products.
Ericsson	37,746	54	80	Public Telecommunication Equipment, Information Systems.
ESAB	4,123	71	91	Welding Consumables (5%), Standard Welding Machines (3%), Mechanised Welding Systems (4%), Gas Cutting Machines (12%).
Esselte	8,734	57	65	Office Equipment, Printing and Packaging, Publishing and Bookshops.
Euroc	3,436	42	56	Equipment for Compaction, Cement, Lime and Limestone, Building Material, International Trading.
Fläkt	7,841	57	77	Environmental Control, Industrial Drying, Air Handling and Ventilation, Fans, Installation Service.
Incentive	3,277	31	59	Heating Technique, Transportation Technique, Measuring Instruments, Biochemistry, Polymer Technique.
Saab-Scania	6,939	18	59	Trucks and Buses, Passenger Cars, Aircraft.

Appendix A *contd.*

Company logotype and name		Employees abroad Number	Percentage of total	Foreign in relation to total sales (%)	Main products (estimated share in world market)
SANDVIK	Sandvik	14,807	58	91	Cemented-Carbide Cutting Tools, Special Steels, Rock Tools, Saws and Other Hand Tools, Processing Equipment.
SKANSKA	Skanska	8,502	31	23	Construction, Civil Engineering.
SKF	SKF	37,472	81	92	Rolling Bearings (20%), Steel Products, Cutting Tools.
SONESSONS	Sonesson	3,518	53	73	Standby Power Systems, Batteries, Railway Breaking Equipment, Pumps, Industrial Doors.
SCA	SCA	5,452	36	67	Pulp and Paper, Sawn Timber, Engineering Products, Hydroelectric Power, Hygiene Products.
SWEDISH MATCH	Swedish Match	11,760	64	75	Flooring, Doors, Matches, Lighters, Packaging Systems, Chemicals.
VOLVO	Volvo (excl. Sonesson)	15,541	22	85	Automotive Products, Energy, Food.

Source: The companies.

APPENDIX B: THE 10 LARGEST FOREIGN-OWNED COMPANIES IN SWEDEN (1983)

		No. of employees	Turnover (Skr billion)
1	Svenska Philips	4,350	3,480
2	IBM Svenska AB	4,021	5,670
3	Siemens	2,827	1,850
4	Marabou (food industry)	2,764	1,410
5	Svenska Esso	2,202	6,640
6	Reckitt-Gruppen (service)	1,925	320
7	Findus (food industry)	1,892	1,120
8	Svenska Knäcke (food industry)	1,653	1,020
9	Svenska Unilever	1,591	1,400
10	Svenska Shell	1,533	8,210

Source: *Veckans affärer* (1984:16, p. 54 and 1984:17, p. 67).

APPENDIX C: THE 20 LARGEST SWEDISH EXPORTERS
(1983)

		Exports (Skr million)	Export/ turnover (%)	Share of total Swedish export of goods (%)
1.	Volvo*	23,130	25.3	11.0
2.	Ericsson*	10,120	39.3	4.8
3.	ASEA*	9,350	30.9	4.5
4.	Saab-Scania*	8,290	39.9	3.9
5.	Electrolux*	6,220	19.4	3.0
6.	Nordstjernan (congl.)	4,690	36.4	2.2
7.	SSAB (steel)	3,950	37.8	1.9
8.	Svenska Cellulosa*	3,800	38.9	1.8
9.	Boliden (copper)	3,640	65.4	1.7
10.	Sandvik*	3,580	35.4	1.7
11.	Statsföretag (congl.)	3,510	30.6	1.7
12.	Billerud (pulp/paper)	2,870	66.9	1.4
13.	KF (congl.)	2,840	11.8	1.4
14.	Alfa Laval*	2,810	30.3	1.3
15.	MoDo (pulp/paper)	2,760	47.6	1.3
16.	ASSI (pulp/paper)	2,740	53.9	1.3
17.	KF Industri (congl.)	2,730	33.9	1.3
18.	SKF*	2,600	16.1	1.2
19.	Svenska BP (oil)	2,600	22.8	1.2
20.	Södra Skogsägarna (pulp/paper)	2,440	57.9	1.2
	Total	104,670		49.8

*Belongs to the group of 20 largest multinationals. See Appendix A.
Sources: *Veckans affärer* (1984:17, p; 52); company annual reports.

188

INDEX

189